DISCOVER MUMBAI

THE CITY'S HISTORY & CULTURE REDEFINED

Shalini Sinha

Marshall Cavendish
Editions

Series Editor: Melvin Neo
Editor: Shawn Wee
Designer: Rachel Chen
Picture Research: Thomas Khoo

All photos by the author except pages 11, 24, 84, 99, 101, 146–147, 155 (Lonely
Plane Images); pages 13, 18–19, 34, 36, 42, 49, 53, 58–59, 70, 80, 83, 86, 108, 111,
114–115, 142–143, 145 (Robert Elliott); page 21 (AFP/Getty Images); pages 48, 88
(Pietro Scòzzari); pages 28–29, 61, 66–67, 77, 79, 96, 129, 132, 134–135, 137, 138–139
(Photolibrary); pages 33, 93, 104, 106–107, 151, 152 (Alamy); pages 3/117, 160 (Asif
Akbar)

© 2008 Marshall Cavendish International (Asia) Private Limited
Published by Marshall Cavendish Editions
An imprint of Marshall Cavendish International
1 New Industrial Road, Singapore 536196

Other Marshall Cavendish Offices:
Marshall Cavendish Ltd. 5th Floor, 32-38 Saffron Hill, London EC1N 8 FH, UK
• Marshall Cavendish Corporation. 99 White Plains Road, Tarrytown NY 10591-9001,
USA • Marshall Cavendish International (Thailand) Co Ltd. 253 Asoke, 12th Flr,
Sukhumvit 21 Road, Klongtoey Nua, Wattana, Bangkok 10110, Thailand • Marshall
Cavendish (Malaysia) Sdn Bhd, Times Subang, Lot 46, Subang Hi-Tech Industrial
Park, Batu Tiga, 40000 Shah Alam, Selangor Darul Ehsan, Malaysia

Marshall Cavendish is a trademark of Times Publishing Limited

National Library Board Singapore Cataloguing in Publication Data

Sinha, Shalini, 1967-
Discover Mumbai : the city's history & culture redefined / Shalini Sinha. –
Singapore : Marshall Cavendish Editions, c2008.
p. cm.
Includes index.
ISBN-13 : 978-981-261-519-0 (pbk.)

1. Historic buildings – India – Bombay. 2. Bombay (India) – Social life and customs.
3. Bombay (India) – History. 4. Bombay (India) – Miscellanea. I. Title.

DS486.B7
954.792 — dc22   OCN244454289

Printed in Singapore by KWF Printing Pte Ltd

Nariman Point,
the "Manhattan
of Mumbai."

CONTENTS

SUBJECT INDEX

❤ Lifestyle

PREFACE

As a rookie Mumbaikar caught in Mumbai's monsoon downpour 18 years ago, I hated Mumbai. India's Manhattan seemed a smorgasbord of multiple-sensory overloads, manic lifestyle, seemingly senseless architectural relics and loads of unputdownable, devil-may-care attitude which Mumbaikars termed *bindaas*. However my Mumbaikar friends loved the megapolis and revelled in the craziness of it all. Mumbai, they insisted, is extremely special. Special because it accepts anybody, says "no" to nobody, and slowly but surely makes an honest Mumbaikar out of everybody.

I could not quite fathom this passion for the city. As I continued to live, work and raise a family there though, I too began to sponge in Mumbai's *bindaas* zing. And while writing the book, I revisited the city I had seen before, crossed before but probably never quite understood and appreciated before. It has been, I'm glad to say, both a pleasure and a revelation. Beneath those mouldy and musty façades I have found a fascinatingly charming and historical city tight rope-walking many crossroads all at once.

Almost like the magician's giant cauldron, Mumbai bubbles and froths as potions of incredible contrasting proportions are thrown in. Name anything Indian and you will surely find it in this cauldron, beginning with the populace itself—the native Koli Mumbaikars, versus the "noveau" Mumbaikars—immigrants from Kashmir to Kerala who, with the city's blessings, are also happy beneficiaries of the Mumbaikar brand.

Of course, each time a new potion is thrown in, the cauldron churns, rumbles and rattles, but given time, mysteriously melds everything together into one amorphous yet somewhat homogenous and happy Mumbai.

No wonder then, when you step into Mumbai you see it all: Mothballed Indo-Saracenic buildings from the British past to the glass, chrome and glitz of 21st-century Bandra Kurla Complex; the human overspill in asbestos and plastic-sheeted shanty towns to space costing approximately Rs. 100,000 per sq ft in the seriously-plush N.C.P.A. skyscraper; and the intensely aspirational roadside shopping of "Fucci", concomitant with an equally aspirational socialite experience in the lavender-infused, exclusive boutiques of international fashion imports, the Breguet, LVMH and JPGs.

In this giant experiment, what tops it all are those two seductively attractive gold-laced potions that heighten the city's appeal. The first is the Indian Stock Exchange, where its seismic shivers are felt by everyone, from industrial giants Ambanis to the modest chawl resident who has investments in meagre Rs. 500 shares. The second is, needless to say, India's most recognisable export and the Indian Dream Factory aka Bollywood. Manned, moved and spawned by millions of noveau Mumbaikars, Bollywood entertains weary India with its unique brand of Indian subculture—a tingling, happy mishmash of all things Mumbaikar and all things Indian.

Incidentally, in the book you will find Mumbai also being referred to as Bombay (the city's pre-1995 colonial name) and its people, the Mumbaikars as Bombayites (the anglicized version derived from the word Bombay). The dilemma for me was to choose what described the megapolis better—the anglicized name Bombay (and its cultural subtext) or the politically-correct, contemporary term Mumbai. Therefore, with mention to the period before its official renaming in 1995, I have referred to the city as Bombay and its people as Bombayites, while the terms Mumbai and Mumbaikars are used when writing on the city in the post-1995 context.

Discover Mumbai is my eulogy to this special city that has also brought some fantastic Mumbaikars into my life. My husband Alok Sinha, the quintessential Bombayite; my two gorgeous daughters, 14-year-old Asavari and 11-year-old Abhisvara, both "genuine", born-in-Mumbai Mumbaikars; Mumbai loyalists and parents-in-laws R.S Prasad and Asha Prasad; and of course my parents—my father R.K.Sinha, who has always insisted that writing books was the way to go for me, and my mother Nishi Sinha, whose passion for words I have obviously inherited. That said, the guidance of Melvin Neo at Marshall Cavendish was no less crucial. Finally, a doff of my cap to one little soldier—a kid called Piyush whom I chanced across in Singapore. I didn't know him much, but saw him fight hard, very hard, to live. He eventually lost the battle to cancer, but inspired me to get up and give life a full shot.

Mumbai is inexhaustible; a lot more could be written about it, but as you read on I hope my modest endeavour with *Discover Mumbai* will compel you to embrace Mumbai as so many others like me have.

Shalinha Sinha
August 2008

AFGHAN CHURCH

You could drive through the cloistered Navy Nagar, Mumbai's hidden bastion of the army and naval bases, and almost completely give it a miss but for the tall yellow steeple which towers over the greenery and landscape.

Sighted from as far as the 1875-built Prongs Reef lighthouse (one of three red-and-white lighthouses located 18 miles out at sea), the Church of St John the Evangelist is known popularly as the Afghan Church. Forgotten for a long time until the Government granted it the status of a Heritage I site, part of the Afghan Church premises has in recent times undergone extensive restoration, breathing fresh life into the monument.

Intended originally as a British garrison church, Afghan Church was built to commemorate the martyrs of the Three Afghan Wars fought in Sindh and Afghanistan between 1835 and 1843, hence its name. The church also commemorates different Indian regiments, including the Bombay Army, the Madras Army and Ranjit Singh's army from Lahore.

Back in the 1820s, the church used to be simply a thatched roof chapel where prayer services were attended by the devout from the "Sick Bungalows" (now known as INS Ashwini, South Mumbai's naval hospital). Henry Moses, a visitor to Mumbai in 1850 wrote about these services, noting that in the "neat little thatched chapel…English service is performed, but all who wish to avail themselves of it must bring their own chairs as it does not contain any seats."

Shortly later, a request by the Bishop saw the start of construction for the Afghan Church, but not before naval officials had promised to erect a church that could serve as a landmark for the approaching Mumbai Harbour-bound seafarers. On 7 January 1858, Bishop Harding consecrated the church.

Like many other churches of its time, the Afghan Church was designed by city engineer Henry Conbeare and architect William Butterfield, well-known for ecclesiastical structures he had architected back home in England.

In its design, Afghan Church departed from other Indian churches built at that time. Instead of materials such as rubble and brick with a layer of lime plaster on it, Afghan Church was given a façade of brown basalt and a limestone spire, complete

LOCATION:

Navy Nagar, Colaba, Mumbai 400005
Tel: 22020420
Catch Bus 123 from Churchgate Station or Regal Theatre and alight at the Afghan Church stop. Open daily from dawn to dusk. If you find the door locked, walk into the verger's home next to the church and he will happily open it for you.

with wide Gothic arches, wrought iron railings and an eight-bell tower. It was aesthetic to the eye and easy on maintenance in Mumbai's notoriously wet and humid weather. And as promised, it sported a steeple that rose a magnificent 210 ft into the sky!

As in most churches, its calm, high-ceiling interiors are a charm. It boasts of beautiful stained glass panels and encaustic flooring imported from England. Sitting in the church, it is difficult to miss William Butterfield's attention to small-comfort details such as wooden choir stalls, chancel furniture and rifle-rests next to the teakwood pews for soldiers to rest their rifles while praying!

Weekly masses continue to be held at Afghan Church.

The high-ceiling interior of the Afghan Church.

AMITABH BACHCHAN

When you say Bollywood, you could say Amitabh Bachchan. Truth be told, it was probably Bollywood fans of Indian, African, Mid-Eastern and Southeast Asian extraction whose zealousness got him voted as the 2000 Actor of the Millennium in the online BBC poll, beating many Hollywood stalwarts. But then, it is Amitabh Bachchan we are talking of—actor par excellence and indisputably the most awesome ambassador of the Indian film industry.

His life story, if ever made into a film, has grand elements of drama, romance, horizon highs, deepest lows and, above all, a never-say-die spirit. At 65, well past the age of running around trees and lusting for the leading nymphet (which he recently did dare in *Nishabdh*), Amitabh Bachchan is the most enduring and visible face of Bollywood. Married to Bollywood actress Jaya Bhaduri and a father of two (one being Bollywood's current hunk Abhishek Bachchan), Amitabh's career graph mirrors in many ways the graph of Mumbai's film industry.

With his deep baritone voice and 6'3" lean stature, the man has charmed all since he debuted rather unnoticeably in 1969 as one of seven characters in a movie titled *Saat Hindustani*. The gawky man suffered rejection at All India Radio, India's single radio channel then, which didn't think much of his sensuous baritone! He was also overlooked for umpteen movies. Then stardom struck. *Zanjeer*, in which he played an angry young police inspector, became a blockbuster, probably hitting a nerve under the turbulent political climes India was then in.

People lapped his anger, nicknaming him the Angry Young Man. In a succession of movies, that character—the humorous, Robin Hoodisque hero taking on the goons and the most eligible damsel of the day took the country by storm. Such was Amitabh's cult following, fans would wait hours to sight him wave from the balcony of Prateeksha, his walled bungalow in Mumbai's northern suburb of Juhu. Anything he did became a style icon. When Amitabh danced a particular way all of India did the same; when he knotted the abnormally long ends of his shirt on a particular shoot, India aped. Bambaiya, Mumbai's local slang that Amitabh's characters spoke in many of the movies, became cool. Amitabh was 'in'...until a series of incidents waned off the superstar's sheen.

At the height of his popularity in 1982, Amitabh met with a freak accident while working. After many months of near-death scenarios, the actor came back, but found that the legions of fans who prayed for his life had surrealistically seemed to withdraw support from his films. Then in 1984 he tried his hand at politics. He won a Parliament seat, but by his own admission was an utter failure. And in 1996 after a failed one-stop entertainment corporate venture known as A.B.C.L., the star was declared bankrupt.

Amitabh thus returned to what he claimed was the only thing he could do best—acting. Yet so edgy was his financial predicament that in an interview he recalled how after suffering sleepless nights he walked up to ace Bollywood producer Yash Chopra, bared his soul and was signed on for *Mohabattein*, relaunching his career at the age of 58. In the next couple of years, his die-hard followers saw, much to their chagrin, their debt-ridden demigod do films and anything else for money—endorsements for soap, hair oil and food, on top of hosting *Kaun Banega Crorepati*, the Indian counterpart of the television show *Who Wants to be a Millionaire*. By 2003, Amitabh Bachchan had successfully and single-handedly repaid a 90-crore loan hanging on his family.

Amazingly, 34 years on today Amitabh is 'in' again. Since 2005, he has been back in films exploring different genres and themes. His movies *Shootout at Lokhandwala*, *Cheeni Kum* and others have resurrected his career with portrayals of what men his age think, behave, look and aspire for. In September 2007, *The Last Lear* premiered amid great curiosity at the Toronto Film Festival. This was Bachchan's 172nd film and his first English-language film. The Phoenix is here to stay.

Amitabh Bachchan (left) receives instructions from the director before a take for the film *Family: Ties of Blood*.

ANGADIAS AND **DIAMONDS**

This could be on *Ripley's Believe It Or Not*. The world may scoff at its naivety, but Mumbai's $10.84-billion international business in diamond processing runs piggyback on an army of domestic couriers called *angadias* who carry no international registration, no special security and no insurance! One of India's largest imports, these cherished blings are also its single largest export. *Angadia* services ferry rough and processed diamonds repeatedly between the cities of Mumbai, the diamond industry headquarters, and Surat, Ahmedabad, Bhavnagar and other diamond processing centres.

Most *angadias* belong to the Gujarati Patel community, and are a 300-year-old carryover from Mughal emperor Akbar's reign when communication across his vast dominion was accomplished by using people as messengers. Today, close to 60 *angadia* firms employing 5,000 people operate out of tiny, rambling offices in Mumbai's diamond district in the Opera House area, which ironically hardly conducts itself with the style and aura you'd associate with this magnitude of business. Buildings are crumbling and noxiously smelly. Swarms of diamond brokers crowd the alleys and lanes spilling out on to the main four-lane road. Most dealers sit at one of the two major diamond office buildings—Heera Panna and Prasad Chambers, each as decrepit as the other.

Notwithstanding all of this, the area does big business in its own unique style. Casual almost to the point of absurdity, diamonds are brought into dealers' offices by thousands of brokers criss-crossing the two buildings. The dealer's requirement for rough or polished diamonds is often scribbled and stuck on a piece of paper on their office doors, which if promising leads to the broker walking in with his pieces. Diamonds, sorted and selected, the deal is done!

Post-dusk, tiny taped paper packets with diamonds worth crores of rupees are sent to the *angadias* along with the only paperwork that is ever done in the whole process—a waybill called a *jhangad*. With packets of diamonds tucked in the insides of their trouser waistbands, the *angadias* take a regular, second-class overnight train to the processing destination. Next day they follow the same route in the reverse, bringing back polished diamonds to Mumbai. Devoid of any armoured security cover or weapon for personal defence, this "no security, no fuss" modus operandi takes you back to the good old days of just a great measure of implicit trust and faith!

ART AT **KALA GHODA**

Quite the nodal point in the cityscape in the last decade, Bartle Frere's British Bombay—the Fort district where Kala Ghoda is located—has risen again in a new avatar as a fashionable and happening art district. The perfect venue for the cocktail circuit amongst all things arty, this area has become even more enticing with the refurbishment of its beautiful heritage structures, bringing out the charm of its nostalgic past.

Kala Ghoda boasts as many as 14 top-end art galleries. Yet not long ago in the 1990s, the district was in a battered state. Other than the well-heeled patronising the area's old-time restaurants such as Khyber, Wayside Inn and Copper Chimney, or browsing for music in the age-old Rhythm House, buildings here were usually populated with tiny stores and office tenements, roads were choked and the area was singularly lacklustre.

That despite the presence of the prestigious Jehangir Art Gallery, a landmark institution on the Indian fine art map. The pioneer gallery, built by Cowasji Jehangir in 1952 to give exclusive visibility to the post-independence Indian arts scene attracted artists, playwrights and intellectuals who came to showcase their art and hang around its socialist café, Samovar, discussing life and philosophies. For lesser-known artists, Jehangir Art Gallery's pedestrian walk was opened up as an Art Walk. Over the years the Art Walk itself has become an institution. Open throughout the year except during the monsoon season, many serious artists have come up from this very modest beginning.

Yet none of this did much for the sagging Kala Ghoda. In 1999, a two-week long Kala Ghoda Arts Festival was launched. The precinct was shut to vehicular traffic and converted into a space where vendors, art houses and folk artists showcased their art. From poetry readings, art and handicraft fairs, dance and music performances to art shows, this art melange had something for everyone. Buildings in the vicinity like the David Sassoon Library, Max Müeller Bhavan and NGMA also hosted events such as discussions and film screenings.

The Kala Ghoda Festival has since become an annual event. And with the vibes back in the air, corporations have offered financing refurbishments and civic maintenance, giving the area that ambience perfect for the art scene.

Kala Ghoda has come full circle. In the British days this was the place to see the glitterati hang out with the literati at the now-dilapidated Esplanade Mansion (across from Kala Ghoda) which used to be the famed Watson Hotel. The resurgent Kala Ghoda has ensured that all art aficionados and glitterati are back toasting to the art, music and high-life that has returned to its precincts.

The following are details of some renowned art galleries:

National Gallery of Modern Art
Mahatma Gandhi Rd
Open Tues–Sun, 11 am–6 pm
Tel: +91 22 2285 2457
Entrance fee for foreigners: Rs. 150

Jehangir Art Gallery
161 Mahatma Gandhi Rd
Open daily, 11 am–7 pm
Tel: +91 22 2204 8212

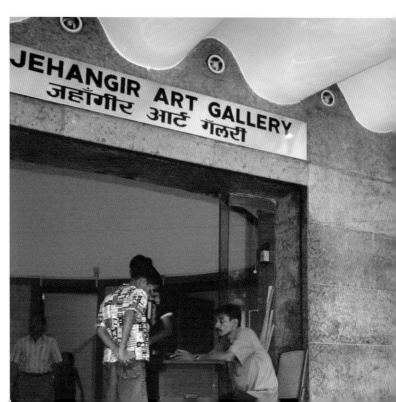

Artists Centre
Ador House, 6 K Dubash Marg,
off Mahatma Gandhi Rd
Open Mon–Sat, 11 am–7 pm
Tel: +91 22 2284 5939

Bodhi Art Gallery
ITTS House, 28 K Dubash Marg
Tel: +91 22 6610 0124

Max Müeller Bhavan
6 K Dubash Marg, off Mahatma Gandhi Rd
Tel: +91 22 2202 7710

Institute of Contemporary Indian Art
ICIA Building, Rampart Row, next to Rampart House,
Open 11 am–7 pm
Tel: +91 22 2204 8138 / 39

ASIATIC LIBRARY AND
THE TOWN HALL

The British left some very beautiful landmarks for Mumbai. This is an edifice to be admired in the stillness of night when all of Mumbai is asleep, the Fort area ghostly quiet and all that's alive is the 170-year-old Town Hall bathed with muted yellow light.

Home to the Asiatic Library, the building has a façade that can kid you into thinking you are in Greece or Rome. All virginal white, the Town Hall is 200 ft long, 100 ft deep and is supported by eight tall colonnaded, ribbed Doric columns. Long wooden doors and tall windows open onto a pedimented portico accessed

Mumbai's most iconic British relic supported by colonnaded Doric columns and a sweeping 30-step flight.

by a sweeping 30-step climb from the road. Undeniably an ethereal nocturnal sight, many a famous Bollywood romance has been shot on these hallowed steps.

Located near Horniman Circle, this grand neoclassical building bags the prize for being one of The Raj's most handsome relics. If you stand on its portico, you can feel its grandeur as it stands heads above the rest around it—the Horniman Circle in front, the Mumbai Stock Exchange diagonally across on its far left corner and The Reserve Bank of India on its right.

Daytime though is quite another story. Harsh daylight, honking taxis, buses and pedestrians swarming out like ants from an anthill crowd around, transposing the edifice and the Asiatic Library it houses within back into bustling, blundering Mumbai.

The Asiatic Library is a veritable treasure trove of unique manuscripts, books, sculptures of forgotten colonial architects of Mumbai and original pieces of literature. The high-ceiling, fan-ventilated dull grey public library in the main town hall is open to all. In those old steel drawers are handwritten, index card-style catalogues you can search for books while your child makes use of the small and rather incongruent colourful children's library section. With prior permission, you can go down the wrought iron divided Regency staircase and see some phenomenal life-size marble statues of British and Indian luminaries such as the legendary Mountstuart Elphinstone who was Governor of Bombay, Sir Jagannath Shankarshet and Sir Jamshtejee Jeejeebhoy, those who made Mumbai the place it is today. Equally impressive is the library's collection of 800,000 antique volumes and over 3,000 ancient manuscripts in Persian, Sanskrit and Prakrit. These include the original *Shahnama of Firdausi* written in Persian in 1853; *Vasupujyacharita*, a 12th century Sanskrit text on the life of Jain Tirthankara Vasupujya; and thousands of old coins (even a rare gold *mohur* or seal belonging to the Mughal emperor, Akbar).

If extremely lucky, you may also get to see the real *pièce de résistance*—one of only two known original copies of Dante's *Divine Comedy*, a leather-bound book, which was donated to the Library by Mountstuart Elphinstone.

LOCATION:

Shaheed Bhagat Singh Marg, Fort (near Horniman Circle), Mumbai 400020. Open Mon–Sat, 10 am–6 pm. Admission is free.

BAL KESHAV THACKERAY

Love him or loathe him, Bal Keshav Thackeray is one unputdownable man. A cartoonist turned politician, the 83-year-old "Tiger" (a moniker given to him by his party followers) may have lost some of his teeth today, but

underestimate him not. Other national political parties chafe dealing with this maverick politician whose grassroots grasp makes him one happy, unavoidable, uncrowned king of Maharashtra. He has never contested in any elections, yet exercises a kind of control over Maharasthrians unparalleled by any other leader. What the man is about is evident from his self-confessed admiration for some of Adolf Hitler's policies in an interview by *Asiaweek*: "I am a great admirer of Hitler…I do not say that I agree with all the methods he employed, but he was a wonderful organiser and orator…what India really needs is a dictator who will rule benevolently, but with an iron hand."

In 1966, Bal Thackeray established his political party, the Shiv Sena, to promote the Hindutva ideology of Hindu chauvinism as well as to protect the "sons of the soil"—the Maharashtrian natives—from the influx of non-Maharashtrian immigrants (Muslims, South Indians, Bangladeshi refugees, the Biharis etc).

Operating out of Sena Bhavan in Dadar, an old Maharashtrian enclave, the Sena has a well-oiled system of *shakhas* (local offices) fanned out in every nook and cranny of Mumbai and Maharashtra, and even some other states.

Yet not all is hunky dory about the Shiv Sena. The party has been accused of targetting minorities, especially Muslims, and Bal Thackeray himself was put in the docks for inciting and activating his *sainiks* (the Shiv Sena workers) into violence during the 1992–93 Bombay riots. Known for his rabid anti-Muslim sentiments, Thackeray had once likened Islam to terrorism, calling on the Hindus "to fight terrorism and fight Islam". However in recent times, especially after the 2006 Mumbai train bombings perpetrated by Islamic fundamentalists, Thackeray was seen to have taken a softened stance towards the Muslims when he praised the city's Muslims for standing up against the fundamentalist Islamists.

Notwithstanding its right-wing political stand, the Shiv Sena is involved with many local civic issues. It has seen a good measure of success in facilitating and allievating the lot of slumdwellers in Dharavi, and also in bringing improvement to the city's infrastructure.

BAMBAIYA

At a vegetable vendor's stall, try asking for *aloo* (potato in Hindi) and the vendor will probably look at you and ask, "Looking for *batata*?" *Batata*, if you please, is potato in Portuguese! And if you try probing errant collegians hanging out at Marine Drive during college hours, you may feel snubbed by their answer, "Boss (used aggressively to address both men and women) *khaali peeli* (unnecessarily) don't get into a *lafda* (trouble) with us…we're just doing time-pass (killing time), yaar."

Forget about trying to deconstruct Bambaiya with some English-Hindi dictionary. Like the city and its people, Bambaiya is a brain-tickling hodgepodge of languages and dialects spoken by the original native Kolis and swarms of migrants to the city.

Comprehending Bambaiya is a cerebral challenge. Words and phrases are peppered with a twist or double entendres and mean something absolutely different from what it could have been in the languages and dialects it came from. Marathi, Konkan, Tamil, Portuguese, English and Gujarati, all have snuck into this genre of Hindi. As a *Wikipedia* entry appropriately explained, just as Cockney and Black American English work vis-à-vis 'proper' English, Bambaiya works vis-à-vis Hindi.

Heard as often on the streets as in the elite company of bankers and hip professionals, the charm of this slang is seeing Mumbaikars across class barriers embrace it. Once comprehensible, Bambaiya has a texture that completely hooks you with a huge dollop of panache. Not surprisingly, what was until recently a language used by the working masses, lackeys and popularised in Hindi movies has become Mumbai's lingua franca. Indeed, Bambaiya can happily claim to be the *baap* (father) of all Indian dialects or slangs today.

Bambaiya is best picked up when you spend time with locals. Try you must, to speak a few words of Bambaiya if you are in Mumbai. Mumbaikars love to hear others speak their way.

If you simply cannot get the hang of it but still want to impress the Mumbaikar friend, forget everything else. Just let him or her know how *mast* (fun) the city is. *Ekdum dhaasu*! That should get you by!

BANDRA

Hidden amidst a warren of lanes, high-rises and incessant traffic noise is a Mumbai from the pre-British days. This enclave called Bandra is located on what once was Salsette Island, beyond Mahim Creek, a 30-minute drive from the southern part of the city. Home to East Indian Christian (ex-Hindu Christian converts originally from Portuguese colonies of Bassein and Salsette who continue to practise many of their original Hindu rituals) and Koli families, Bandra in its nooks and crannies has an ambience and flavour that is sure to transport you to the past when palm-fringed rice farms and fishing boats dotted the landscape.

Bandra used to be a cluster of 25 *pakhadis* or hamlets of which a few exist even today. Notable amongst those are Ranwar behind Mehboob Studio, Chambai, Shirly-Rajan, Pali and Chuim (which now falls in neighbouring Khar). Inhabitants of these areas were once fishermen or farmers cultivating rice and a sweet variety of onions which could be seen hanging from many of the homes.

The British also settled here, the posh Pali Hill fringed with palms and mango orchards serving as luxurious settings for their homes. In fact the British established Bombay's largest 18-hole golf course in a large portion of the Chuim Greens and called it

Bandra's ubiquitous crosses erected to ward off evil, a sign of mixed beliefs of ex-Hindu, Christian converts originating from erstwhile Portuguese territories.

the Pali Hill Golf Course. Later Bandra saw another round of residents coming in—Parsis and other immigrants who escaped from the city's overcrowded areas. These days Bandra is a typical cosmopolitan residential area with people from all parts of India and religious leanings living together.

Bandra's beauty lies in the small cluster of traditional residential villages. Best showcased in the enclave contained within the heritage churches of St Andrews, St Peters and Mount Carmel, here you'll see tiled, single and double-storey cottages fronted with deep verandas, low windows and grill staircases. Outside homes, the Portuguese-Christian influence stares from residents' nameplates with surnames like Pereira, Fonsecan and Pessoa. Note the wooden crosses planted randomly outside homes, at junctions of three roads (probably superstition-driven), at burial grounds and even at what would have once been the sea front. These are mute reminders from a century ago when the calm and idyll Bandra fought in a very God-fearing Christian manner to ward off the dreaded plague and other ghostly spirits.

Just as those crosses stand as reminders of Bandra's past, so too do the other famous landmarks—the Mount Mary Church and the remnants of the Castella de Aguada or Fort of the Waterpoint—the fort where a fountain (*aguada*) provided fresh water to Portuguese ships sailing these waters. Built by the Portuguese in 1640 and known simply as Bandra Fort, most of the fort precincts were demolished by the British when they took over these islands. Yet the fort walls still stand tall with a stone plaque inscribed with details of the fort. It is quite a charmer and you may find film and music video shoots going on in its vicinity.

If you want to catch the evening sun set on the water and intermingle with Bandraites (as the residents call themselves) you should head to the refurbished popular promenades at Carter Road and Bandra Bandstand. Bandstand, located on the tip of the Bandra promontory, is in fact also the venue for the annual "Celebrate Bandra" festival of music and dance.

Honestly though, most visitors come to Bandstand not as much as to gawk at the fort or the church, but at Bollywood star Shahrukh Khan's palatial home—Mannat, a pristine white heritage mansion once called Villa Vienna, that he bought at a rumoured $22 million!

BANGANGA **TANK**

By the time the waves of the Arabian Sea curve around the Bay to the northernmost tip of the promontory, you find yourself 15 m above sea level at Walkeshwar, the highest point in Mumbai. The name Walkeshwar is derived from the Sanskrit name for an idol made of sand, *Valuka Iswar*. Hindus believe that its history goes back 5,000 years when Lord Rama, standing here, worshipped a self-fashioned sand idol of Shiva the Destructor.

LOCATION:
Walkeshwar Road,
Malabar Hill

Legend has it that when Rama, the exiled prince from the epic *Ramayana*, was on his way to Lanka to free his abducted wife Sita from the demon Ravan, he was advised to perform a prayer ceremony at this high spot. Overcome by thirst and unable to locate fresh water so close to the sea, Rama shot an arrow into the earth and out sprang fresh water of the Ganges. Christened Banganga (Ganga or Ganges from the *bana* or arrow), this freshwater pond today provides a rare link to Bombay's ancient past.

Walkeshwar houses a Shiva temple complex as well as the Banganga Tank. The Walkeshwar Shiva Temple and the Banganga Tank were first constructed in 1127 during the reign of the Silhara kings. However, Portuguese plunderers demolished the temple when they ran over Bom Baia (the name they gave the city). Later in 1715, local philanthropist Rama Kamath financed the reconstruction of the temple complex. Both the temple and the tank have since been restored, and smaller temples such as the Venkateshwar Balaji Mandir (1789) and Rameshwar Mandir (1825) have come up in the surrounding area.

Driving down the main road, one may often miss this tranquil oasis if not for the façade of the temple. Adjacent to the Shiva temple down a long flight of stairs is an old walled rectangle pond on the right. In olden times, oil lamps were lit on the two pillars that flanked the entrance. Walk through this entrance and you find yourself on the Banganga Tank steps. From here on, a continuous flight of stairs from all sides leads to the water's edge. In the middle of the tank the odd, tall wooden pole that stands out rather awkwardly is symbolic of the centre of the earth that Lord Rama's arrow had pierced.

Interestingly, a minute's walk on the left of the Banganga entrance behind the row of low-rise houses brings you face to face with the Arabian waters against lashing the coastline!

Do not be surprised if on an early morning visit to the Tank you sight *sadhus*, Hindu mendicants and common folk engrossed in elaborate ceremonies and meditation postures. Banganga's western bank houses a branch of the Kashi Math, a Saraswat Brahmin sect of *sadhus*. Banganga is still used for prayer ceremonies. In keeping with the Hindu tradition of taking the blessing of Mother Ganges for all important events—births, deaths, full moon, new moon and special festival days—Mumbaikars come to Banganga for the blessings of Mother Ganges.

In recent years, the Banganga Tank has also become the venue for the annual Banganga Hindustani classical music festival, an extremely popular event held in February.

A Hindu ritual in progress in the middle of the tank. Notice the bamboo pole symbolic of the earth's centre pierced by Lord Rama's arrow.

BEACHES OF MUMBAI

Mumbai without its beaches is a city without its soul. Not only for the fish their waters provide the Koli inhabitants, but equally important, much of Mumbai's history and present-day complexion is intimately linked with visitors who have come to the city via boats from distances far out across the seven seas.

Chowpatty and Marine Drive are Mumbai's most-photographed beaches, but there are other beaches that deserve mention because they offer interestingly alternate perspectives to the city.

Juhu Beach is suburbia's Chowpatty, with the same street food, *kulfi* (creamy ice-cream, Indian style) stalls, cackling kids, strolling grandparents, love-lost couples and hordes of noisy people. Located in the affluent suburbs of Juhu, Andheri and Santa Cruz where the famous names of Bollywood reside, the Juhu Beach waters are just as they are always shown in all Bollywood flicks—worth a little toe-dipping while holding your love's hand, but "unswimmable". Also, with the whole world and

People young and old enjoying a day at Juhu Beach.

its cousins here on the beach, you obviously cannot strut in your two-piece or dream of lying around acquiring the bronze! You come here essentially for an evening out with friends and family, watch the sun set on the ocean and catch a good wholesome round of *pav bhaji* (be warned: mind your stomach!).

Manori, Gorai, Madh, Marve—a train or car and a ferry ride away, this is the cluster of beaches where you head to sample authentic Koli fish delicacies amidst palm-fringed environs and sun-drying *bombil*. About 90 minutes from Mumbai, it is calm and far away from the chaotic madness of the megapolis. The TV sets and cars notwithstanding, here Koli villages exist in their natural surroundings just as they have done for so many centuries that they called the seven islands their home. Film personalities and big industrial corporations own bungalows in this vicinity which they use for weekend retreats. For the tourists, simple Spanish cottage-style resorts sprinkle these beaches, and Kolis also have shacks to rent out to those who may want to "sack out" on a more modest budget.

BEST BUSES

Lest you get all hot under the collar after a trip on one of these buses, please be reminded that while they have happily ferried people for close to a century, they don't claim to be the best. It is just that their name—Brihanmumbai Electricity Supply and Transport, abbreviated to BEST, stands for Mumbai's transport and electricity providers!

Between the trains and the BEST buses, Mumbai can be mapped efficiently. The buses connect the southern tip of the city to its northernmost shores till Navi Mumbai, Thane and Mira-Bhayandar in Greater Mumbai. Though slow during the rush hours, for a large population of Bombayites BEST buses offer a comfortable, organised and economical alternative to the jam-packed train travel. They are manned by a uniformed bus driver and conductor, the latter notoriously temperamental, who may be heard screaming, "*Pudhe chala!*" or "Move forward!" in Marathi, as he 'tick-ticks' his clicker and issues tickets to passengers while walking up and down the aisle of the bus.

BEST, an autonomous body run by the Municipality, was set up in 1873, and it introduced its first bus services on three limited routes in Bombay on 15 July 1926. Such was the demand that the services, meant originally for rush-hour office goers, soon had to be increased. By the end of that year, around 600,000 people had been transported via BEST buses. Today, 3,400 BEST buses run over 340 routes in Mumbai and 4.5 million Bombayites commute annually on them, making them one of Mumbai's indelible leitmotifs.

If you are one of the out-of-towners stumped by the various kinds of buses and the different categories that you see them split into, here is the demystification mantra.

Buses that you see plying on Mumbai's roads are mainly single-decked, though BEST also runs double-deckers and even a number of vestibule buses. Generally, bus services are split into five categories. The ordinary services have buses that stop at every bus-stop, and they are spotted with a white-coloured route number displayed against a black backdrop. Limited services stop only at the more major bus-stops, and they don red-coloured route numbers written on a white backdrop with the word 'Ltd' suffixed on them. The specials, which only ply on select routes, can be identified by white-coloured route numbers on a red background, while the express services ply on long-distance, intra-city routes and have their routes displayed in red on a yellow background. Finally, the air-conditioned buses are identifiable by their route numbers starting with the letter 'A'. Tickets are priced between a minimum fare of Rs. 3.50 for an ordinary bus trip, Rs. 5 for a limited bus trip and Rs. 22 for the air-conditioned service.

For your added convenience, BEST maintains Internet websites where you can chart your itinerary and plan your trip: http://www.bestundertaking.com/transport/Area.asp and http://www.mumbai-central.com/buses.

BHABHA ATOMIC **RESEARCH CENTRE**

Scientist Dr Homi Jehangir Bhabha once voiced his hope, saying, "When nuclear energy has been successfully applied for power production in, say a couple of decades from now, India will not have to look abroad for its experts but will find them ready at hand." Indeed, today India has a completely home-grown nuclear programme, thanks to the vision of that one scientist.

LOCATION:
Trombay,
Mumbai 400085
Tel: 25505050 / 10
Website: http://
www.barc.ernet.in

The genesis of this self-sufficiency lies in the early 1940s when a soon-to-be independent India was coming to terms with severe poverty, illiteracy and population crisis. Under those circumstances came a visionary in Bhabha, who thought beyond the immediate issues and realised the immense potential of nuclear energy as an alternative source for electric power generation.

On 19 December 1945, on Bhabha's initiative and with the financial support of Sir Dorabji Tata Trust, the Tata Institute of Fundamental Research (TIFR) was inaugurated in Mumbai, launching the Indian nuclear research programme. It was only in 1957 however that the Atomic Energy Establishment Trombay (AEET) began operations in its own dedicated premises in Trombay, which was then a sparsely-populated fishing village called Turbhe. AEET was rechristened as the Bhabha Atomic Research Centre (BARC) in 1966 as a tribute to Dr Bhabha after he was killed in a plane crash.

Fitted with cutting-edge laboratories facilities and equipment, and manned by the top scientists, it is at BARC that India's major nuclear research has taken place. BARC also has several nuclear reactors—Apsara (1957), CIRUS (1960), Purnima I (1972), Purnima II (1984), Dhruva(1985), Purnima III (1990), Kamini and the now-defunct ZERLINA.

The institution is renowned internationally for its multidisciplinary research in the fields of nuclear reactor design and installation, fuel fabrication and chemical processing of depleted fuel. In recent years BARC has also become involved in biotechnology research, and has a great measure of success in the development of disease-resistant and high-yielding variety of crops, the most famous being groundnuts.

BARC, taken between 1957 and 1961 when construction was just completed.

Meanwhile, the erstwhile fishing village of Turbhe where it all began is now a bustling suburb and home to Anushakti Nagar, a full-fledged residential complex where BARC employees stay.

BOLLYWOOD

For all the talk about the Indian film industry being the poorer copycat cousin of Hollywood to the point of its mishmash name Bollywood (the Hollywood of Bombay), check this out.

Long before the West saw Shakira's shimmying prowess, Bollywood's pinup moll Helen had shaken it all in cabaret song sequences outfitted in innumerable navel-revealing, feathered leotards. Before *Titanic*, the "ultimate" tragic tale of love, Bollywood already had its own epic in the 1960 film *Mughal-E-Azam*, a tale of commoner Anarkali's unrequited love for Mughal Prince Salim. And long before *Chicago* and *Moulin Rouge* introduced the musical genre in legit contemporary film lexicon, the Hindi film industry had adopted, adapted and exulted at the box office with its own desi brand of film vocabulary, mandatory with song, dance, colour, drama and melodrama.

Fullbodied desi, the Hindi film industry located out of Bombay works on numbers too boggling for most film industries across the globe. In 2006, Bollywood produced 800 movies. With one billion Indians, it is estimated that one in six persons on this planet watches Indian movies, and spends close to Rs.100 (almost a day's salary for many) on these Bollywood flicks each month. Bollywood revenue figures may pale in comparison to

LOCATION:
Film City, Goregaon

those of Hollywood, but the Hindi film industry also spends a fraction of the budget for a Hollywood production.

With a surge in international interest, some Indian movie-makers, aspiring to break into the West, have begun exploring cinematic content differently. Nevertheless it is the typical Bollywood flick that sells by the barrels. Dubbed rather disparagingly as "*masala* mix", this cinema represents mainstream commercial narratives. These are the movies that spin cinematic magic with Greek god-like Hritik Roshan and ice maiden Aishwarya Rai romancing in Rio with lip-synced singing and dancing against psychedelic studio sets as well as a generous dollop of drama with a villain, a vamp and 20 lackeys.

Structurally, Bollywood filmmaking is rather *hat ke*, a pet Bollywood catchphrase for anything different. It requires not only the regular team of actors, director, scriptwriter and cinematographers, but the crew includes the dialogue writer, lyricist, music director, singers and dance directors.

Of course, mainstream movies could be made without dance numbers, but without dialogues and music? It's a challenge! Bollywood icons such as lyricist and dialogue writer Javed Akhtar, singers Lata Mangeshkar and Asha Bhosle, music director O.P. Nayyar and scores of others from these fields have become household names just doing that part of the Bollywood job.

With the help of modern technology, publicity and marketing, movie honchos ensure that catchy dialogues and music tunes of forthcoming movies are disseminated as widely as possible via radio shows, DJ remixes, mobile ring tones, and television and promotional advertisements. If successful, people are already primed for the movie when it hits theatres. Western sensibilities may find this paraphernalia over the top, but all major Hollywood studios—Warner Brothers, Paramount, Walt Disney, Sony Pictures and Universal Studios—are tying-up with Indian film companies.

There is obviously an acknowledgement of the commercial success of Hindi films. They are world-class, stylised and slick; stunts are neat, sound and cinematography proficient, and production systems have been streamlined over the last decade. Amazingly all of this $1.2-billion business comes right out of suburban Mumbai. Inconspicuously dotting the northern parts of the city are over two dozen state-of-the-art film studios, post-production facilities, as well as animation and music recording studios. Off a highway and in the forest cover of Borivali National Park is Mumbai's biggest film studio, Film City—so inconspicuous you almost miss the board announcing its precincts. Out of bounds without prior permission, close to 20 shoots go on simultaneously at the sets and outdoor locations within its compounds.

Why Mumbai is called the dream city (*maya nagari*) is visible here. Drawn by Bollywood dreams, the city sees an influx of Bollywood-crazy wannabe stars, songwriters, singers, directors and dancers everyday. A fistful make it to the top and find their fancy plush cars, their entourage of exclusive staff and crazy fan followings. Bollywood's celebrated star Shahrukh Khan came to Bombay with no sugar daddy, yet such is his popularity that today he is called King Khan. Still most other strugglers hooked onto their celluloid dream fall on the wayside, eking out a hard living as "extras" (junior artistes needed for every song, wedding and fight sequence).

But nobody complains. Mumbai never sends you back. It is said of this city that it embraces every dream in whatever capacity it can, just as Indians embrace the Bollywood dream in whichever manner it spins. Irrational, fool-hardy and *karma*-dependent it may sound, but this is the ultimate story of hope, dreams and lives lived passionately.

Crowds at the Regal Cinema catching the latest Bollywood flicks.

CENTRES OF **EXCELLENCE**

All too often we associate Mumbai with Bollywood and the stock exchange. Much as these are the most celebrated icons of Mumbai, the city is also home to internationally reputed educational institutions which, by virtue of their performance and celebrated alumni, rank amongst the country's best.

LOCATION:

Indian Institute of Technology Bombay Powai, Mumbai 400076 Tel: 25722545

Indian Institutes of Technology, Bombay

The famed Indian Institute Technology, Bombay (the institute continues to call the city Bombay, not the new-age Mumbai), or IIT-B as it is happily abbreviated, is one among a chain of seven autonomous engineering schools located across the country. IIT-B is situated 18 miles from South Mumbai overlooking Powai Lake in the northernmost suburbs of Mumbai.

This engineering institute makes it to this collection of uniquely Mumbai icons not only because IIT-B is the second-oldest campus among the IIT colleges, having just completed 50 years, but it has also wrestled up the ranks and is being touted as the IIT *numero uno*, pipping IIT Kanpur. Recent surveys have found that backed by fantastic academic mentoring and an accomplished bunch of ex-IITians, IIT-B has become the choice of almost half of the top 100 students that pass the rigorous CAT engineering entrance exams. Incidentally, out of the lakhs of engineering aspirants that take this gruelling exam across India, only 5,000 make it through to pursue their education in engineering under the IIT umbrella of elite institutions.

Some IIT-B trivia: The department annexes are connected by a corridor called the Infinite Corridor, and the Tansi House is a hostel exclusively for married research scholars. Famous names among its alumni are Nandan Nilekani (co-Chairman of Infosys Technologies Ltd), Victor J. Menezes (Chairman, Board of Governors, APEC and ex-Senior Vice Chairman of Citigroup) and Arun N. Netravali, an Indian-American engineer and businessman who is a pioneer of digital technology including HDTV.

St Xavier's College

If IIT-B is the engineering mecca, then Xavier's Mumbai, as collegians fondly call this institution, is paradise for the humanities and science stream students. Located in the vicinity of South Mumbai's Metro area and accessible by local trains and buses, Xavier's is counted amongst the country's top performers.

Dedicated to St Francis Xavier, a 16th-century Jesuit saint, the college has been in operation for close to 150 years. Started in January 1869 by the priests of the Jesuits order, a Christian religious group that spearheaded modern English education across the length and breadth of the country, St Xavier's College is best known for combining the spirit of education with a holistic development of its students. Many renowned administrators, film-makers, journalists and theatre personalities have passed through the corridors of the historic Indo-Gothic building the college is housed in.

Some St Xavier's College trivia: Its vibrant annual college festival, Malhar, is on the must-do list for all collegians. The college's favourite hangout is called The Woods. Amongst its famous alumni are ace cricketer Sunil Gavaskar, internationally-celebrated music conductor Zubin Mehta, ad man Alyque Padamsee and actress-activist-politician Shabana Azmi.

LOCATION:
St Xavier's College
5 Mahapalika Marg,
Mumbai 400001
Tel:
22620661 / 2 / 5

CHAWLS AND WADIS

This is where the average Mumbaikar lives.

Just as strong is Mumbai's association with its glitterati, so is its intimate bonding with the *wadi* and chawl mandals (social groups living in the chawl and *wadi* settlements). In the Mumbaikar's lexicon, concepts of individualism, privacy and nuclear are as alien as they are second nature to the glitterati living in splendid isolation. Many strong Mumbai icons like the festival of Ganapati Puja, Janmashtami and even Bambaiya, Mumbai's slang so happily adopted and popularised by Bollywood, are cultural by-products of these semi-urban Mumbai settlements.

A product of the 1920s cotton and industrial boom era, the chawls were actually British barrack-like tenements. Constructed initially by private entrepreneurs and later by the Mumbai Development Department, the intention was to accommodate the droves of migrant labour that came to work in Bombay's industrial belts. Over time, their families came in, and paucity and prohibitive cost of larger spaces forced these families to continue living in those tenements. Slowly that became a pattern of life—crowded but cosy, convenient and in many ways, rather addictive.

The chawls are stubby, rectangular three to four-storey blocks with narrow, drab building entrances and single-room tenements of 12 x 18 x 10-ft space with a tap in one cranny, a kitchenette in another nook and a common, shared toilet down the corridor. Entire families sleep, cook, eat, study and live in this one room. Lives are in fact lived more in the common access "gallery" (colloquial term for corridors) outside than in the confines of the one-room homes. The gallery, leading to the shared toilet as well, usually flanks the street. It is in these galleries that family members, herded in different groups, spend entire days. Walk into one of the chawls and you see young adults hanging out, senior citizens gossiping and playing cards, and the women spreading laundry, sewing and rolling *papaddums*.

Often, the privately constructed chawls provide for a central courtyard space flanked by chawls on all sides, while those built by the Bombay Development Department are designed to have free spaces between buildings. Both serve as communal spaces where weddings, festivities and other community events are held. Not quite a pleasant thought, is it? The book *Bombay: The cities within*

talks about chawls having 300 to 400 single rooms which could accomodate up to 900 families! The lifestyle that has spun off this social fabric is implanted yet impressive, contrived yet cohesive. Living in such incestuous proximity, its dynamics are such that it has been the subject of research by sociologists and urban town planners, and even been romanticized in the candyfloss psychedelia of Bollywood flicks.

Today, gone are the cotton mills and the arbitrary Rs. 50 per room rents (the Rent Control Act putting a more realistic perspective on rentals). The chawl buildings are in a derelict condition. With Mumbai housing as expensive as New York, the government wants to now put them on its heritage list but hungry builders are waiting to replace them with modern skyscrapers.

WADIS

Despite carrying the age-old label of being India's skyscraper city, many of the native Mumbaikars have spent a generation or two in these abodes before moving into more urban apartments.

Translated literally, *wadi* means an orchard. Amid Mumbai's urban jungle it is very easy to miss these stuffed-in-a-nook urban villages sprinkled in the olden part of the city, but look hard. From Girgaum to Parel, you will come across housing clusters named Fanaswadi, Gaiwadi, Keshavji Naik Wadi, Ambawadi, Kumbharwada, Koliwadi, Dhobiwadi, Kotachiwadi and many others, built in a similar fashion.

Communal living
in Mumbai,
chawl style.

The names, all suffixed with *wadi*, refer either to the caste, community or religious leanings of the original inhabitants or to an iconic connection with the *wadi*. Therefore, cow heads (*Gai* is Hindi for cows) on the gate's pillars gave the name Gaiwadi while Khot's initiative in the creation and subsequent sale of Kotachiwadi homes gave this cluster its name. Influenced also by their resident composition, the *wadis* exhibit unique architectural nuances such as Portuguese-Christian décor and Hindu icons.

Like the chawls, the *wadis* also spawned their own semi-urban culture. In the past, during Diwali, *wadis* would be dressed in synchronised *kandeel* (paper lantern) lights and the residents would organise sports and games competitions—badminton, table tennis and the space-saving *carom* taking the pride of place. Like the chawls, they also had their own *sarvajanik* (community) festivities of Ganapati Puja and Janmashtmi, where the highlight would be an evening showing of a Hindi movie flick on a *parda* (makeshift white cloth screen) in the courtyard of the *wadi*. In fact, the Sarvajanik Ganapati celebrations that so typify Mumbai's community festivities today was first introduced by the freedom fighter Lokmanya Tilak in one of the Girgaum *wadis*, the Keshavji Naik Wadi.

What best exemplifies the *wadi* architecture and culture is Kotachiwadi. Walk down through the lane past the red-and-white-coloured St Teresa Church in Girgaum and you will find yourself staring at the 150-year-old Kotachiwadi—a tranquil cluster of antiquated, low-rise double-storeyed houses inhabited by East Indian and Goan Christians. Brightly coloured in warm reds, yellows and blues, these Portuguese-style residences are embellished with beautiful wooden railings, verandas and staircases. Owned by East Indian Christians, Kotachiwadi's residents were originally fisherfolk who became Christians under the Portuguese influence, and followed Portuguese customs, languages, dressing and lifestyle. Homes here are distinctly Christian as is obvious from the Bible plaques on some main doors as well as the residents' nameplates.

In this mini-Lisbon of Mumbai, only some 28 of the 65 original houses are left standing today and are protected as a heritage precinct. If you are in this area, remember to wind up your tour with a meal at the restaurant Anantashram, renowned for its unique coastal cuisine eaten in these East Indian homes.

CHATRAPATI SHIVAJI **MAHARAJ**

This is the man who swung in the concept of Maratha Pride in every Maharashtrian soul. This is also the name that you come across on most of Mumbai's important landmarks.

Chatrapati Shivaji Maharaj, whose name sits on the erstwhile VT Station, the Prince of Wales Museum, the Sahar International Airport and other important post-colonial landmarks, was the Maratha king who dared to raise his hackles against the mighty Mughals and established, for the first time in Maratha history, an independent Maratha Kingdom.

Born in 1627, Shivaji inherited his father's strong independent streak. By 1674 Shivaji had fulfilled his dream and established an independent Maratha Empire, wrested over from the dominant Mughal Empire and the Sultanate of Bijapur. The moniker, Chatrapati (meaning chief, or King of Kshatriyas, the protector of his people) was bestowed on the king at his coronation on 6 June 1674, which was sanctified and presided by a Brahmin priest from Varanasi.

Known for his guerrilla warfare tactics that best suited the rugged, mountainous Deccan Maharashtrian terrain, Shivaji evolved into an able, benevolent and just administrator. Today, such is his iconic stature that Shivaji Maharaj is featured in textbooks, and his exploits are part of popular folklore.

The statue of Chatrapati Shivaji Maharaj.

COLABA

On the extreme southern tip of Mumbai, starting out at Regal Cinema and going down beyond Navy Nagar lies Colaba, a narrow, talon-like strip of land jutting out into the Arabian Sea. Colaba at the start of the Causeway has traditionally been the tourist-hippie hangout. Cafés, drugs, hostels and loads of touristy shops populate this area. Yet as you go deeper into Colaba, the area reverts to typical Mumbai with residential areas, schools, temples and locals busy with their daily grind.

How that strip evolved into a mishmash of tourist icons, art-deco buildings, residential, skyscraper clusters and office district needs telling as it fashioned most of what you see today as contemporary Mumbai.

In the early days, Colaba used to be two islands called Colaba and Old Woman's Island. Koli fisherfolk populated its coast and many of the local fishes like *bombil* (the famous Bombay Duck) were found in abundance here. These islands belonged to the Portuguese who, by signing the Treaty of Bassein in 1542, had received them from the powerful Gujarat-based Sultanate of Cambay.

Just as marriage brings in change, a dowry deal definitely did so for Colaba's fortunes. In 1662, the Portuguese gifted these marshy islands in dowry to the British Emperor Charles II when he married the Portuguese princess, Catherine of Braganza. The dowry was passed on but for over a decade after that, Portuguese officials in Goa and Bombay resisted the transfer, until exasperated, Charles II rented out Colaba to the British East India Company in 1675. General Aungier, the Governor of Bombay and the President of the East India Company's Surat factory took possession of Colaba, paying a rental of a mere £10 per annum. (Today, real estate in Colaba costs 2,000 to 3,000 times that!)

Colaba languished though. In 1743, General Aungier tried a more respectable deal, leasing it out to an antiquarian, Richard Broughton, for Rs. 200 per annum. Fortunes did not change much until 1796 when Colaba became a cantonment.

What did eventually bring in the moneybags was an upbeat economy and connectivity that was established over three episodes of Backbay reclamation. In 1838, the Colaba Causeway was completed, linking for the first time the smaller islands.

The second round of connectivity came between 1917 and 1929 amidst The Great Depression and a botched-up Backbay reclamation scheme. It was an ambitious plan to reclaim 1,500 acres of land on the western shores of Colaba, but this had to be whittled down due to various issues. That said, Mumbai got its Marine Drive and the land between Churchgate and Colaba, though not quite the way it had been envisaged.

The final round of reclamation came in the 1960s and 1970s. It gave to Mumbai what is nowadays regarded as a huge town-planning monstrosity—the infrastructure-deprived office district at Nariman Point and the adjacent Cuffe Parade, the residential skyscraper cluster west of Colaba choking with narrow roads and minimal green cover. Imperfect yes, but this congestion, living cheek-by-jowl and unending demands on one's sensibilities is what makes Mumbai a concentrated melting pot.

Roads filled with heavy traffic, a common scene at bustling Colaba.

 COLABA **CAUSEWAY**

Souvenir T-shirt vendor in Colaba Causeway.

Behind the Gateway of India and the famed Taj Mahal Hotel lies Colaba Causeway, dubbed the Oxford Street of Mumbai. Populated by a melange of the moneyed old timers, young tattooed sleazy mavericks and the mundane Maharashtrian, this causeway maintains an almost nonchalant existence and presents a succinct snapshot of Mumbai on the edge.

In the 1950s and 1960s Colaba Causeway was the trendiest place for shopping and the place to spot Bombay's coiffured ladies and their entourage. Today that aura may have faded, but depending on which part of the causeway you are in, you will still be assured of excellent ethnic bargains, big brands, varied fresh produce and Mumbai's best *ganja*, gal or guy, if you so fancy!

Strangely, as you take in Colaba Causeway from the Gateway end and proceed deeper into the southern part, the sights and sounds change dramatically, almost as if revealing Mumbai in tableaux. Starting from Regal Cinema, an impressive art-deco relic of the 1930s and 1940s, it is that part of Colaba Causeway that backpackers, hippies and other experimental travellers love to frequent. Sold as a romanticized la-la land for the ultimate anonymous, hedonistic escapades, the causeway is populated by cafés, Irani joints and local fare restaurants.

Saunter down the causeway in the winter or monsoon months and you will hear languages as alien to you as the faces and nationalities they belong to. This stretch is a popular pick-up point for anything cheap—drugs, food, hookers and seedy accommodations located in decrepit old buildings in the back alleys. There are also mid-priced garment and shoe boutiques and pavement peddlers of hip fake antiques, jewellery, T-shirts and other bric-a-brac.

Further up the scene changes subtly. The hustlers make way for chic boutiques selling branded garments, toys and other equally mundane products. The imposing gated compound of the Parsi-owned elite Cusrow Baug, a charming Parsi enclave and the adjacent BEST Bhavan, known earlier as the Electric House, dominate the skyline with a very well-attended Hindu temple on the other side. Mumbai's first horse-drawn tram cars introduced in 1873 by Stearns and Kitteredge were housed in the same place where Electric House stands today. Today, BEST runs the 2,000-strong fleet of Mumbai's buses from this stone fronted building.

Here ends touristy Colaba. As the Mumbaikar's Colaba rolls in, the snapshot changes dramatically. The causeway narrows down, and slip roads named curiously as Pasta Lanes get more congested. The satchel-saddled, school-bound kids jostle for pedestrian space with handcarts, fishmongers, cycles, BEST buses, perpetually honking black and yellow taxis, and of course, the unwieldy number of swanky chauffeur-driven private vehicles.

Colaba in this part is dominated by Colaba Market, famous for its vegetable vendors. It is not an easy place to negotiate, but does give you a peek into ordinary Indian lives. Homes that you see are small, cramped and shabby. From the variety of ordinary homewares and odds and ends displayed in the shops, you know its clientele are not necessarily the well-heeled. It is a marketplace, like most others, with traditionally-clad, ornate nose-ring et al, ferocious Koli females hustling their fresh fish catch. Cotton pillows and mattress fluffers, butchers, tailors, local grocers, kitchenware stores and even a quaint and well-stocked embroidery store exist cheek-by-jowl. The real gems though are the couple of hole-in-the-wall, unimpressive looking antique sliver shops like the one called Silver House. Its superior quality, well-crafted pure silver merchandise is in great demand with the genteel socialites of South Mumbai.

Visit Colaba market, if you can muster enough love for the place, during the festive seasons of Janmashtami and Ganapati Puja. All dressed up, noisy and more than a wee bit chaotic, this is the time when the entire community comes out on the streets to participate in the festivities.

But when the causeway beckons both foreigners and locals, it does so not only for esoteric exotica but also for food and more food. Colaba has many eateries, each with its own quaint stories attached.

The cafés at the mouth of the causeway, Café Churchill, Café Royal, Café Mondegar and Café Leopold, were empty units remodelled by Irani immigrants into cafés and restaurants selling typical Parsi and Irani fare. In their most contemporary avatars many of these are snazzy joints—Café Mondegar, made famous by a juke box and the Bombay-themed wall mural painted by well-known cartoonist Maria Miranda; and Café Leopold, with Elvis poster, draught beer and a cult status. Then there is Bade Miyan, located in the back alleys with its finger-licking *baida rotis* and *kababs* dished out from what used to be a food stall; Delhi Durbar and its Mughlai-style *biryani* and *kadai* chicken; Paradise Restaurant, still selling what it always did to the generations of happy customers that have patronised it—wholesome Parsi cuisine with *salli boti*, *dhansak* and *kheema pav*; homestyle Goan food at New Martins' Lunch Home; and finally, *chaat*, *pakoras*, thick mouthfuls of seductive "slurpillicious" *lassi* and *jalebis* at Kailash Parbat.

Colaba's latest claim to fame is the novel *Shantaram*, Gregory David Roberts' international bestseller about Mumbai and its curious underbelly. The book is set in a large measure in Café Leopold. In operation since 1871, Café Leopold was a dubious hippy hangout until it became an inadvertent hero in the novel, now being made into a Mira Nair Hollywood film starring Hollywood's Johnny Depp and India's Bollywood icon Amitabh Bachchan.

Café Leopold, a popular dining place among tourists.

CRAWFORD **MARKET**

One of the championing outposts of British architecture in Mumbai, Crawford Market deserves a look, not necessarily for what it sells today, but for what it represents of British India.

Mango wholesalers at work in Crawford Market.

Renamed Mahatma Jyotiba Phule Market after a leading social reformer, this used to be Bombay's wholesale market up to the last decade. Located at a busy traffic intersection north of VT Station, every conceivable fresh food product from fresh poultry, meat and fish at its butcheries, to fresh fruits, veggies, a variety of dried fruits, bake ware and cane knick-knacks can be bought within the compounds of this busy market.

During summer, hordes of diamond-dripping, chauffeur-driven Gujarati housewives haggle for crates of Alphonsos, Western India's favourite mango. There is also a section that sells pets, which in the past had come under flak for supposedly being a smuggled animals' racket. Back in the days before liberalization, Crawford Market was the place to find imported, sometimes smuggled Kraft cheese, olive oils, pasta sauces and Hershey's chocolate syrup for that posh Italian dinner you were preparing. That business has dried up, as has the market's status as the premier fruit and veggie wholesaler of the city but Crawford Market limbers on.

Victorian in its spirit, this Mumbai Heritage building, completed in 1869, is located behind the Fort area. In 1862, after the Fort walls had been ordered to be torn down, Arthur Crawford, the new Municipal Commissioner, set out to improve the civic infrastructure. The area was developed into huge market covering 72,000 square yards and named after him. A classic colonial edifice, the architect William Emerson infused it with an amalgam of Flemish and Norman architectural styles, using coarse Kurla stone along with eye-catching red stone. A fountain inside the building (you may have to look hard for it at the Venubhai Vithal Morde stall under boxes of fruits!) and the bas-relief just above the entrance depicting farmers working in their fields was designed by Lockwood Kipling, father of famous novelist Rudyard Kipling, who worked at J.J. School of Art across the road. Interestingly in 1882, Crawford Market made news as India's first building to be lit by electricity.

The market opens daily at sunrise and continues to be a favourite haunt for both locals and visitors to the city.

CRICKET

God help you if you arrive in Mumbai during the Indian cricket season, which is practically all the months minus the monsoon seasons! Billboards, TV and radio programmes, roadside vendors, *maidans* (parks) and open spaces—it's cricket everywhere. Each cricketer is lauded or shredded (depending on his kismet for the day), every sixer and every fielding slip discussed, as if its outcome could potentially tilt the earth's axis.

Not that the rest of India doesn't care, but Mumbai cares more—it has after all given the game some of its best players. Sachin Tendulkar, who holds the world record for the most number of Test cricket centuries; Sunil Gavaskar, considered cricket's finest batsman; along with Ajit Agarkar, Pravin Amre, Vinod Kambli and Sanjay Manjarekar all belong to Mumbai. More interestingly, most of these ace cricketers owe their careers to the same cricket training ground, the hallowed Shivaji Park Gymkhana in the residential suburb of Dadar in North Mumbai.

Mumbaikars are obsessed about cricket. Due to a paucity of space, no outdoor sport other than cricket and monsoon soccer thrives here. On roads between buildings, gully cricket is played

Gully cricket in action as Mumbaikars develop a passion for the sport from young.

on makeshift pitches with tennis balls plastered with insulation tapes. At the August Kranti *maidan*, Oval and Cross *maidans*, cricket is played passionately by umpteen groups of sweaty boys hogging the grounds running between wickets and pitches.

At Shivaji Park though, grounds cricket is played seriously and professionally. Cricket lore has it that Sachin Tendulkar's coach Ramakant Achrekar got him to change school and move to this neighbourhood just to train at the Shivaji Park grounds. Vinod Kambli, another cricketer, used to commute a good 15 km by local train to get to Shivaji Park for training.

Created in 1925 by the Mumbai Municipal Corporation, Shivaji Park derived its name from the statue of Shivaji Maharaj (the great Maratha king) placed in the precincts of the park. Spread over 70 acres, 1.3 km in circumference and roughly the size of four football fields, Shivaji Park is like a neighbourhood park. On its fringes are children's play areas, a walking track and a low parapet where groups of seniors citizens, teenagers and toddlers with their mums and helpers hang out in the evenings.

But beyond all of this, the rest of the park is a cricket training ground. No distractions, no walkways, no interruptions. There are about 30 nets belonging to coaches and clubs such as Western Railway, Young Mahim, Regal Club, Bharat CC, Mahim Juvenile and Shivaji Park Gymkhana, where training sessions are organised for boys of different ages. Chalk-a-block with trainees dressed in cricket gear, games are played simultaneously on the nets and it is quite a sight watching the frenzied scramble between wickets and fielders of different teams often getting all mixed up. Equally inspirational is catching professional cricketers having a game on these pitches—a huge experience for the little aspirants.

Of late, this park has lost some of its sheen due to intermittent political rallies held here. Yet, Shivaji Park remains the undisputed cricket nursery of India. And Mumbai, the cricket-crazy city.

In September 2007, Team India landed in Mumbai after a surprise victory in the first World Twenty Championship held in Johannesburg. It was a working day, but the city poured onto the roads, offices shut down and Mumbai stopped work for those few hours as players were ferried in a procession from the airport to the Wankhede Stadium for a felicitation ceremony—all because their boys had brought the cricket World Cup home!

DABBAWALLAHS

Again, you'll find this in Mumbai and nowhere else. Critics have pooh-poohed it for being blown out of proportions, but fact remains that Mumbai's *dabbawallahs* (literally, men who carry *dabbas* or lunch boxes) have been rated by *Forbes* magazine with a Six Sigma (99.99 per cent accuracy) performance rating, which means that just one error occurs in six million transactions—on par with giants like Motorola!

Dabbawallahs are a 5,000-member strong cooperative run by a bunch of Maharashtrian semi-literate men earning between Rs. 3,000–5,000 per month working as lunch meal couriers. For the last 125 years, they have functioned as the home-grown variants of modern-day courier companies.

The logistics are simple. From across the megapolis, 250,000 cooked lunches prepared by housewives and home-based caterers are packed in aluminium lunch boxes and ferried daily via foot, trains, cycles and handcarts.

Executed with military precision and punctuality, the lunch boxes reach out across the city to offices goers in a good old relay-like system aided to perfection by the Mumbai railway system and the city's linear layout. For Rs. 300–350 ($6–7) per *dabba* per month, *dabbawallahs*, working in teams of four, pick up tiffins from homes and commute via local trains to the railway station closest to their receiving client's destination. There, in just 10 minutes, *dabbas* are sorted, placed in rectangular trays each accommodating up to 40 *dabbas*, and transported on handcarts, in time for the client's lunch. Once lunch is over, the same route is followed in reverse order.

Impressively, at the core of the *dabbawallahs*' efficiency and near-perfect success rate is a bizarre codification system comprising of alphabets, colours and numbers scrawled on the lids of the *dabbas*. Demystified in business school studies, it turns out this mishmash, constructed by illiterates, has a rather scientific method in madness. The net portal http://www.successfulmanagers.com explains the code system, citing an example: "In code 3MC4 10D, 3 stands for number of the carrier who delivers the *dabba* in the Nariman Point area, MC denotes the office in Mafatlal Centre and 4 is for the floor the receiver's office is located on. In another code below, 10 is the code number

for Churchgate station where the tiffin is offloaded and D for Dahisar station where it was collected."

Simple, effective and efficient. However, with changing eating habits and the provision of canteens and eateries within many of the office premises, the *dabbawallah*'s livelihood is being threatened for the first time in its 125-year-old history.

Notwithstanding this, the *dabbawallahs* so impressed Prince Charles when he visited them while on a trip to Mumbai a couple of years ago that for his wedding to Camilla Parker Bowles, these *dabbawallahs* were amongst the handpicked Indians who were extended a wedding invitation!

Military precision delivery of *dabbas*, or lunch boxes.

DHARAVI

If Mumbai is India in a microcosm, Dharavi is hinterland India in a petri dish. Squeezed into 1.75 sq km, Dharavi sits in the heart of Central Mumbai, skirting the Mithi River and wedged between the central and western railway lines. Dubbed as one of Asia's largest slums, peer beyond the shanty town and what you will see most surprisingly is Dharavi the "enterprise town".

Dharavi had not always been a slum. In the early 20th century what was once a fishing village got swamped over as the first wave of industrialisation swept into Mumbai. Dharavi gradually became the marshy swamp where everything from unwanted waste to unwanted humans—convicts, bootleggers and hapless immigrants—was unceremoniously dumped. Today, that marshy swamp is the life breath of more than a million of Mumbai's dispossessed and migrant masses who come searching for the Bollywoodisque *sone ki nagari*, the city of gold. When the gold chase becomes a mirage, Dharavi embraces, giving hope for life and the spirited drive for the next full meal.

Beyond the squalor and grime, the spirit of Dharavi is mesmerising. There are no idle gawkers, no beggars. Instead one encounters the Rs. 10-a-show pirated movie shack, the cacophony of uniformed school children in the dozen or so schools, the barber's shop and the doctor's clinic. While native Marathi women huddle at the community water tap washing their laundry, others make *papad* in their homes. At the other end you see workshops involved in multifarious businesses—the Gujarati potters with their kilns afire, tailoring units housed in makeshift duplex spaces churning out 200 shirts a day, *zardozi* embroidery units manned by skilled Muslim craftsmen from Uttar Pradesh, workshops of recycling units, leather tanneries, jacket and bag makers, soap makers, fabric dyeing units, wholesale grain merchants and an assortment of other skilled and unskilled service industry personnel.

Virtually every business venture finds its space in Dharavi. One study boasts of this slum supporting roughly 15,000 single tenement business units in its clusters. Dharavi has probably best been described by a journalist as a conglomerate of "unregulated, unorganised business clusters". If numbers are any measure, this shanty town generates businesses worth over a staggering

LOCATION:

Dharavi is best visited with boutique tour companies like Mumbai Magic that give you a personalised tour of the place. Contact Deepa Krishnan at +91 9867707414. Email: deepa@ mumbaimagic.com

$1 billion! It is estimated that 80 per cent of its residents are gainfully employed, earning salaries between Rs. 3,000–15,000 monthly. And as a testament to its financial strength, the Indian Bank opened its first ATM in Dharavi in February 2007.

The leather industry alone does business to the tune of $750 million exporting a majority of its products. In fact, any belt or handbag picked up in the international market could have been made in Dharavi! Between its tanneries, manufacturing and export units and leather retail businesses located on the Sion-Dharavi edge, the industry employs over 200,000 people. The other big money spinner is the recycling business, employing over 250,000 people and processing 80 per cent of Mumbai's recyclable waste.

Organised in a zone-like manner within Dharavi, industrial units and cottage industries stand cheek-by-jowl. Recyclers, as workers of the recycling units are called, are located in what is called the 13th Compound. A walk through the place is a

A shop peddling movie magic in Dharavi.

revelation. Inside workshop after workshop, junk is stripped, pulverised and refashioned into something else—some by machines like smelters, others by sheer sweat-dripping muscle work. And this process is followed time and again!

Elsewhere, tanneries operate. Though largely illegal establishments (since most tanneries have officially shifted to the outskirts of Mumbai), work carries on unhindered. The air is thick with the nauseating smell of salting raw hide, vats of colour and ammonia, but work goes on. Close by, bags, belts and jackets get fashioned in similar tenements.

In another cluster you will encounter the cottage entrepreneurial units—the fabric dyeing units with big dyeing vats and bales of coloured cloth hung up to dry, the *zardozi* embroidery workers, tailoring units, all working out of their home-cum-workshops; and snack, savoury and *papad* makers. Finally, there is the *kumhaarwada*—the potter cluster, manned by Gujarati potters, many of whom have been residents of Dharavi since 1918!

It is a busy place indeed. Life here is seen at its harshest, where bowels are emptied in one toilet shared amongst 1,400 of its residents. Other than the much celebrated 60-Foot Road and the newer 90-Foot Road (these incidentally are the names of the roads—a hint probably of the profundity of those sizes for Dharavi residents?), lanes between homes are non-existent, walking as you do placing your foot in the narrow spaces along the walls on either side of open drains with water flowing between your legs below.

Homes at their affluent best are *pucca* (concrete) structures of one-room tenements within which families of five to six adults and children sleep by night and cook, eat, work and watch TV (almost a must for every well-heeled Dharavi resident) during the day. For the more fortunate registered residents, amenities such as water and electricity are provided. Most homes, though bare, are clean and well-appointed, equipped with a refrigerator, colour-TV set and stoves.

At its worst, life is a lot more grinding, with asbestos, plastic and tin sheets making up hovels running on water and electricity pilfered from those few legitimate main spigots installed for the residents. Despite the harsh sunshine, many of these tenements are so tightly packed in that only slivers of natural light can peep in.

Each of these hovels, not to be trivialised by its looks, provides a sheltered space to the 10–15 people it is sublet to, who sleep and use it in shifts, when the other lot is at work. Come daytime, sleeping mattresses are stacked up, the tenement is cleared up and work begins all over again.

Today, this enigma is attracting a lot of attention. In an attempt to beautify Mumbai, Dharavi is at risk of being demolished and taken over by property developers. For the charm of having their privacy restored with private bathrooms and running electrical and water connections, residents are being offered a mere 225-sq ft apartment space, often smaller than their current space. Essentially, a higher-than-usual FSI (floor space index) offered to potential developers has resulted in apartments getting pigeon-holed and squeezed together. Prime Mumbai land will then get freed up. Avaricious private developers are already queuing up, hoping to grab their pot of gold.

Yet, for all the green grass on the other side, those who live in Dharavi are in no hurry to pack up and move.

Vignettes of Dharavi residents at work.

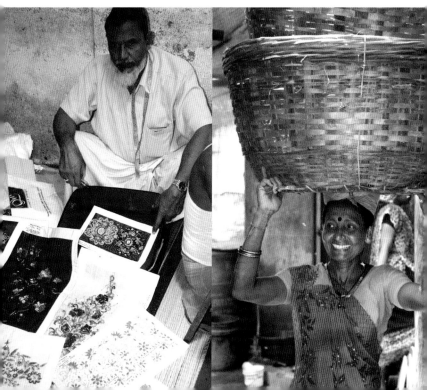

DHOBI GHAT

Quite like Morocco's Fes leather tanneries and their dyeing vats (minus the olfactory assault), Mumbai's iconic Dhobi Ghat is apparently the world's largest open-air laundry.

Most locals would never venture here (it is just another place of work after all!), but tourists love it. What you will see are rows of open-air concrete wash pens with flogging stones; and across the sky, criss-crossing rows of linen, almost bunting-like, hanging

LOCATION:

Dr. E. Moses Road (Saat Raasta near Mahalakshmi Station)

on strings pegged to wooden poles.

   Laundries of the traditional Indian kind, this is where close to 200 dhobis (washerfolk families traditionally involved in laundries) work, cleaning linen and garments from Mumbai's hotels and homes. You will come across vats of caustic soda used for soaking stained clothes and others with soapy, sudsy water for soaking soiled clothes. Between the flogging, wringing, drying and ironing of clothes, it is one gem of a photo opportunity cashed in even by Bollywood for dramatic hoodlum chases and a very hummable song sequence filmed for a recent blockbuster, *Lage Raho, Munnabhai.*

FLORA FOUNTAIN

What does Flora Fountain, a water fountain adorned with an ornately carved statue of the Roman Goddess Flora, happen to be doing in the business district of South Mumbai?

With innumerable small businesses as well as major foreign banks housed in many of the old, refurbished, heritage buildings in its vicinity, Flora Fountain is quite the hub of South Bombay today. Sitting in the Hutatma Chowk Square at a junction of five roads where the Bombay Fort originally stood, the Flora Fountain graces the popular Fort area. Many a Bollywood "cops-`n-robbers" potboiler has been shot around this colonial relic. Sculpted out of imported White Portland Stone in 1864, the fountain depicting the Roman Goddess of Flowers was commissioned by the Agri-Horticultural Society of Western India for a whopping sum of £9,000. Although built in honour of Bombay's then Governor Sir Bartle Frere (credited with Bombay's urban planning in the 1860s), the Flora Fountain curiously found no mention of Sir Frere by the time it was inaugurated.

Today, it jostles for visibility with Hutatma Chowk, the square it sits on. In 1960, following a troubled phase in a violence-fraught creation of the state of Maharashtra, a black stone Martyr's Memorial was erected adjacent to the Flora Fountain to honour those who lost their lives in the movement.

On a weekday, the area surrounding it, known as the Fort or the Fountain area, has a buzz seen in few other places. Not only does it draw people working in the business district, but bargainers—students, workers and a multitude of others—also converge for different purposes.

Fountain is the destination you head for if you are looking for cheap China-made electronic goods, second-hand (and often pirated) books on anything from architecture to Archie Comics, music and the latest pirated software, which vendors sell along the pavements and lanes of the Fountain area. Quaint buildings on roads snaking on either side of the Fountain also house delectable local food joints that serve the best of Malvani, Maharastrian and Udupi and Continental home-style food.

On many a day, the Fountain is also the venue for protests and processions by trade unions, lobby groups and various other disgruntled masses.

Vying for attention—the contemporary Martyr's Memorial and colonial Flora Fountain.

FROM BHELPURI TO **BROWNIES**

Credit Gerald Aungier, the British Governor of Bombay, for the city's food fare. In the late 1600s his grand designs for converting the marshland into a rocking city ushered in the potpourri of peoples, cultures and quirky food habits.

So while the native fisherfolk with their strong "fish palate" sun-dried the odorous *bombil* fish and added it into every curry and meal, the Parsis slapped an egg on almost anything they cooked. Iranis baked breads and biscuits, Muslims fashioned *biryanis* and meat-filled *parathas* while the Chinese refugee-immigrants spiced up their bland Hakka and Cantonese cuisine with desi panache.

Likewise, the homely *dosa* and *idli* morphed into a slick, desi McDonald's-style business proposition. Gujaratis and Marwaris focused on elaborate home cooking and shunned any contact with meat while the Jains, it turned out, were even more finicky vegetarians, shunning all tubers, onion and garlic!

The immigrant Gangetic belt North Indians, with their passion for *puris* (puffed fried bread) and all things fried and zippy on the tongue, developed their own repertoire of snacks laced with chutneys and the Sindhis from post-partition Pakistan brought in their fried and Sindh-style, to-die-for rich cuisine.

With so much variety, what evolved in Mumbai is a mishmash of cuisine styles, cut and pasted to suit the rush-rush existence of the city that never ever sleeps. Behind many of these idiosyncratic options is the expediency of time and money but the bottom line always is that these are easy and quick-fix one-dish preparations with an eye on the pocket and a palate that pleases almost everyone who picks them up.

Along the way, some of these Udupi, Indian Chinese and Irani cuisines have actually spawned into very successful businesses. The famous Chinese *gaadis*—mostly-red vans complete with painted dragons, bizarre Chinese names to match and Nepali chefs masquerading as Chinese—have for years been dishing out Nepali-style noodles, seafood, chicken and veggies with wholesome *masala*, Indian style. A whole new vocabulary of dishes has blossomed under a legit cuisine called Indian-Chinese, and restaurants such as chef Nelson Wang's posh China Garden, a high-end spinoff of the Chinese van, has created a million-dollar empire out of his creations, the *Veg Manchurian* and *Kung Pao Potatoes*. More modest Udupi restaurant chains have also experimented with *idlis*, *dosas*, *sambhar* and the lowly *uttapams*, all tweaked with western ingredients such as cheese, chocolate and various *masalas*.

Irani joints mostly occupy the ground floor corners of buildings which, because of local superstitions, had originally been sold to the immigrant Iranis at throwaway prices. Iranis turned them into classic cafés and rolled out a new trend. Queer and colonial with high ceilings, trademark bentwood furniture, marble-top tables, old grandfather clocks and pictures of the Zoroastrian preacher Zarathustra hung on the walls, these languorous cafés are past good times but they plod along, resisting change as long as they can.

Nevertheless, the food there is oh-so-lip-smacking! The list is such a turn-on: Bachan's *berry pulao* (cooked with the finest of berries imported from Iran) and *dhansak* available at the 83-year-old Britannia & Co. at Ballard Estate; *patra ni machchi* (fish cooked in a leaf) at Jimmy Boy Café at Fort; Kyani's *kheema pav*, Irani *cha* and *brun maska*; and melting warm bread puddings and ginger biscuits at Yazdani Bakery, probably the oldest Irani bakery in the city. Beyond these biggies are also the other no-frills, speciality restaurants without which Mumbai's culinary pilgrimage is never complete.

Shop selling *pav*, **Mumbai's staple food.**

For "fishaholics", a must-try is Mahesh Lunch Home (a little tacky but great for its crabs) or the more upmarket Trishna, famous as much for its Hydrabadi-style black pepper fish as for the quick rum and cokes it dishes out. It may seem quite touristy, but its food is superlative, and you will not come back nursing a stomach on the run. Also mandatory is Gajalee Coastal Foods for its killer delicacy, the Bombay Duck; and Anantashram, written about as much for the old-world ambience of the area it is located in as for the awesome coastal food it serves. Get to Anantashram early though, because if food runs out even just halfway through its opening hours, you may find an impudent 'Closed' board hung on the door!

For Sindhi food, look to Kailash Parbat, an unpretentious sweetmeat and savoury shop where staffers dish out *ragda* pattices, *chaat* and sugar-heavy *jalebis* and *gajar halwa* (a carrot pudding). At the Gateway of India is the iconic roadside stall Bade Miya, poshed-up in recent years, where city visitors and bachelors gorge on *kebabs* and *roomali rotis* served either in their cars or on foldable furniture lining the street. Interesting experience, easy on the purse but not quite guaranteed on quality and hygiene.

Finally, some other equally interesting pit stops: Prawn *koliwada* from Sion; Lokhandwala's Natural Ice Cream with fruity flavours and no egg preparations; *paan* (betel leaf, lime and nut post-meal digestive) from Muchchad Paanwallah (named after the *paan* vendors' legendary moustache) at Breach Candy; *chaat* and Gujarati snacks at Swati in Tardeo, *thalis* at Rajdhani, awesome brownies at Theobromas in Colaba and a Muslim Bohri tiffin at Masala Craft at the Taj Mahal Hotel.

If you have managed to trawl through all of these places, then Mumbai truly belongs to you! Listed below are some popular eating haunts:

Bade Miyan
Tulloch Road, Apollo Bunder, Behind Taj Mahal Hotel
Tel: +91 22 2284 8038, +91 22 2285 1649

Britannia & Co.
Open 10 am–3:30 pm
Sprott Road, Ballard Estate.
Tel: +91 22 3022 5264, +91 22 2261 5264

Trishna
Open 12 pm–3:30 pm; 7 pm onwards
Reservations essential
Birla Mansion, Sai Baba Marg (next to Commerce House),
Kala Ghoda, Fort
Tel: +91 22 2270 3213, +91 22 2270 3214

Mahesh Lunch Home, Fort
8B Cawasji Patel Street, Fort
Tel: +91 22 2287 0938

Mahesh Lunch Home, Juhu
Juhu Tara Road
Tel: +91 22 5572 0059

Gajalee
Phoenix Mills Compound or Kadambari Complex
Hanuman Road Vile Parle (East)
Tel: +91 22 2838 8093, +91 22 2822 6470

Anantashram
Open 11 am–2 pm; 7 pm–9 pm
4 Kotachiwadi, Girgaum

Kailash Parbat
A taste of Gujarati   Open daily, 11 am–11 pm
fare at Tardeo's   Sheela Mahal, 1st Pasta Lane, Colaba, Mumbai -5
Swati Snacks.   Tel: +91 22 2284 1972, +91 22 2287 4823

GATEWAY OF INDIA & THE TAJ MAHAL HOTEL

If the Thames has the Big Ben and the Buckingham Palace manning its waterfront, then Mumbai has the Gateway of India and the Taj Mahal Hotel. Out from the Arabian Sea as you approach the Apollo Bunder (*bunder* means harbour in Marathi) in Colaba, the mighty arch of the Gateway of India and the stately Taj Mahal Hotel rising tall and big in the sky magnificently proclaim: Welcome to Mumbai!

A fantastic amalgam of the Indo-Saracenic and Muslim architectural influence, the Gateway stands 26 m above ground level

LOCATION:

The Taj Mahal
Palace & Tower:
Apollo Bunder,
Mumbai 400001
Tel: 66653366
Nearest station:
Churchgate

View of the Taj Mahal Hotel (left) and Gateway of India (right) from the sea.

with the central dome measuring 15 m in diameter. Solid pillars and arches frame intricate latticework which is topped by four turrets. George Wittet was its designer and Gammon India Ltd, an engineering firm established in 1919, constructed the monument.

A prominent inscription on the Gateway arch pompously informs all visitors that the arch was conceived to receive King George V and Queen Mary on arrival for the Delhi Darbar in 1911. On 31 March 1911, the foundation stone for the Gateway was laid. However, by the time the King and Queen landed in India later in the year, all that could be hurriedly put together was just a papier-mâché structure!

In yet another piece of irony, the Gateway actually saw the exit of the British. On 28 February 1948, after India's independence, the last of the British troops from the First Battalion of the Somerset Light Infantry passed through the archway and embarked on their journey back home to England, marking the end of the British's 200-year rule over India.

Unarguably, a great deal of thought had gone into presenting The Gateway of India as an impressive icon of the British Empire. Between 1915 and 1919, Apollo Bunder was refashioned to align the sea wall so that it would have a wide esplanade with the Gateway sitting at the head of the *bunder*. The Gateway of India was finally inaugurated by the Viceroy of India, the Earl of Reading on 4 December 1924.

Completing the Apollo Bunder snapshot is the equally imposing and iconic Taj Mahal Hotel adjacent to the Gateway. Built in 1904 by the ambitious Parsi industrialist Jamshedji Tata, the hotel owes its origins to an episode when JRD, as the industrialist was fondly nicknamed, was denied entry at the Watson Hotel, Bombay's posh British-style hotel, on account of him being brown-skinned. Terribly humiliated, JRD vowed to build a hotel that would beat Watson in style and grandeur. A British architect was commissioned and he mailed the plans from England. Based on those designs, Hotel Taj Mahal was constructed at a phenomenal cost of £500,000. Sure enough, Watson eventually became history while the Taj created its own, becoming a legend of sorts.

Inspired by the grandiosity of the Taj Mahal of Agra, this hotel is an elegant product of Moorish, Oriental and Florentine architectural styles, described often as an East-meets-West edifice. Rumour however was that the Taj façade design had been inadvertently mixed up and that the waterfront façade was actually meant to be the rear side. Nevertheless, the Taj awes every visitor not only with its impressive pigeon-speckled turrets, cupolas and oriental façade, but also with its opulent interiors dressed up with alabaster ceilings, onyx columns, a cantilever stairway and an eclectic collection of Indian and European arts and artefacts.

Ranked 16th in the *Condé Naste Traveller's* first ever Gold List 2005 in terms of location, the Taj Mahal Palace & Tower in Mumbai has hosted an international jet set—from Bill Clinton and Prince Charles to Mick Jagger, Jaqueline Onassis and Elvis Presley.

For lesser mortals though, the Gateway and its sea-fronted promenade offer a favourite spot for families and tourists to take in views of the monuments, and also to board excursion boats to the Elephanta Caves from the steps behind the Archway. Touts and hustlers hang around the area soliciting business, from selling grass to offering interesting female company and even instant photographs with the Gateway as a backdrop, but they are best ignored. Focus instead on a roasted corn-on-a-cob, and if possible, hop onto the Victoria (the horse carriage, a Raj relic, that you will see strutting the esplanade) and take a ride. Though not quite the original, it may still inspire some royal vibes in your bones!

A Victoria horse-drawn carriage offering visitors a ride.

Also not to miss is the black statue of the Maratha King, Chatrapati Shivaji Maharaj, almost challenging the colonial edifice with Maratha pride from its vantage point in the garden across the Taj.

HAJI ALI **DARGAH**

If you drive past Worli Seaface on any evening, stop and watch. When the sun stoops to kiss the waters of the Arabian Sea your eyes will naturally be riveted towards a white mausoleum floating in the choppy waters. It seems almost on its own, caressing the shore yet not quite there. On clearer days and during low tide, you will also notice at a distance a snaking swarm of people trudging across to the mosque through a rough, bony finger-like concretised strip, the lone kilometre-long causeway that connects the mosque to the Mumbai shoreline.

LOCATION:
Mahalaxmi
Nearest station:
Mahalaxmi

One of Mumbai's most famous Islamic shrines and landmark, this is Haji Ali Dargah, a tomb honouring the Muslim Sufi saint Haji Ali. Constructed in 1431 by his followers, the *dargah* sits 500 yards from the Worli coastline and is accessible only from Mahalaxmi during low tide.

Legend goes that Haji Ali was a wealthy merchant who, after renouncing his material possessions, travelled to Mecca. Confusion prevails as to what happened thereafter. Folklore suggests that the saint passed away in Mecca, but mysteriously, his body was found floating in a casket at the very same spot that the *dargah* stands today.

Like most Muslim mausoleums, this *dargah* stands out for an all-whitewashed look, a central dome and an 85-ft-tall solitary minaret. Within the 4,500 m compound stands a mosque with Haji Ali's tomb. As per tradition, a rich red-and-green *chaddar* (embroidered throw) drapes the tomb, which lies encased in a silver frame. Gilded in psychedelic mirror-work with glass chips of various hues are marble pillars that support the silver frame. Significantly, the pillars have 99 names of Allah engraved on them. The colourful *chaddars* that you see hung across the exterior side façades of the mosque are offerings by the devout. Seeking the Sufi saint's blessings, it is common practice for devotees to press their foreheads to the *chaddar* on the tomb and while inside the *dargah*, pray in separate men's and women's enclosures. Inside the mosque men are required to wear a *gahfiyyah* (crocheted prayer cap) or a handkerchief tucked behind their ears, and women should be dressed modestly with their heads covered.

Venerated both by Muslims and non-Muslims, Thursdays and Fridays are the busiest days for the *dargah* as it sees close to 40,000 people walk down the causeway to pay respects to Haji Ali. If you plan a visit, remember to bring something to cover your head. The narrow causeway can be intimidating as it is lined with beggars waiting for alms (it is prudent to carry loose change that you can distribute on your way out) and shops selling religious offerings. The *dargah* though is a beauty.

Haji Ali Dargah was last given a facelift in the 1960s, but excessive exposure to salinity in the water has put a question mark on its longevity. In fact, the Dargah Trust, which annually earns about Rs. 30 lakhs from the mosque, has sought permission from the government authorities to raze and rebuild the mausoleum. Nevertheless, Haji Ali continues to be one of Mumbai's must-visit spots.

A Haji Ali visit is best concluded with (what else, some more food!) a juice and pizza slice at the Haji Ali Juice Centre located at the entrance to the causeway.

J.J. SCHOOL OF **ART**

LOCATION:
DN Road, Fort,
Nearest station: VT
Website:
http://www.
sirjjarchitecture.org

Ace luminaries from the Indian art scene such as internationally renowned painters M.F. Husain, S.H. Raza, Atul Dodiya, film maker-actor Amol Palekar and many more, have walked the grounds of this hallowed campus. We are talking here of India's oldest and most prestigious art school, J.J. School of Art, located on the heritage stretch between VT Station and Crawford Market on Dadabhai Naoroji Road.

What started out as one school essentially to teach painting and architecture is today an umbrella institution affiliated to the University of Mumbai. Encompassing three distinct entities—the Sir J.J. School of Fine Arts, College of Architecture and Institute of Applied Art, in March 2007 the school inaugurated its post-centennial celebrations, having completed 150 years of existence as an art school.

J.J. School of Art traces its origins to India's First War of Independence, or The Sepoy Mutiny of 1857. In 1878, with a donation of Rs. 4.71 lakhs from shipping magnate Sir Jamshedji Jeejeebhoy, the J.J. School of Art was set up in the building where it still sits today. The recently refurbished Victorian building, built again in a British, Gothic-Revival style of architecture, is surrounded by a sprawling, verdant campus with a century-and-a-half old trees. In fact, the refurbished J.J. School of Art building has won the UNESCO Asia-Pacific Heritage Award for Culture Heritage Conservation.

An interesting point of interest at J.J. School is a metal plaque on a stone-and-wood colonial bungalow informing visitors that the bungalow was the birthplace of Nobel Prize winner Rudyard Kipling, the man who gave us *The Jungle Book*. Rudyard Kipling was born here on 30 December 1865, and for the next six years lived in this tree-lined leafy cottage. It turns out that Lockwood Kipling, the first principal of J.J. School of Art who was also associated with the design execution of Crawford Market, VT Station and the University Buildings, was Rudyard's father!

Encouraged by Kipling enthusiasts, the Maharashtra Government has announced that the cottage, inhabited currently by pigeons and in quite a state of disrepair, will be refurbished and opened by 2009 as a museum housing the rare paintings and sculptures that lie stacked in old dusty storerooms of the art school.

KALA GHODA HERITAGE WALK

LOCATION:
Kala Ghoda,
Esplanade Road
Nearest station:
Churchgate

Dubbed by the colonial city planners as the Crescent for its ideal location and lapped by the wide sea expanse on both sides, the British created in Kala Ghoda an absolute architectural delight. Many of the best buildings of British Bombay were built here and it showcases the evolution of the Indo-Saracenic design trend which sought to blend typically British design elements with traditional Indian styles.

While the picturesque Crescent no longer exists, the best way to experience this area is to walk from Madame Cama Road, and skirting the Regal Circle (also called the S.P. Mukherjee Chowk), walk onto Mahatma Gandhi Road, which during the 1800s formed the ramparts of the Fort area and went by the name of Esplanade Road. Sitting right at the mouth of the Mahatma Gandhi Road is the present-day National Gallery of Modern Art (NGMA, formerly the Jehangir Cowasji Hall), which merits a look not only for its fantastic art exhibitions but also for its 1911 horseshoe-shaped design with the central domed feature. The NGMA, now cleverly restored while maintaining the original façade, is a perfect example of Mumbai's success in preserving its heritage architecture.

Across the road is the Indo-Saracenic Prince of Wales Museum built in 1914. Even if you do not fancy a museum walk, this edifice will intrigue you because it is a delightful fusion of what the British architects aspired and longed for—their home in the islands of Europe; and what they saw and worked with—the idioms and materials procured from this tropical and sunny paradise.

If you walk further down through the porticoed building archways opposite Jehangir Art Gallery and cross over to the triangular parking lot, you will find yourself standing smack in the middle with Rhythm House, the decades-old music store, on your right and the busy road chock-a-bloc with traffic in front of you.

You are now at Kala Ghoda. Translated in English it literally means the Black Horse, popularly named so because it once sported an imposing 13-ft bronze statue of King Edward VII astride a black horse. Installed in 1879, the statue sat there marking the change in the Fort skyline until post-independence 1965 when, along with other British-era reminders of a similar nature, it was relegated to the Bombay Zoo, the Jijamata Udyan. Today, Kala Ghoda retains its name even though there is no *ghoda* (horse) in sight.

Across the Kala Ghoda are the other noticeable Crescent structures—Elphinstone College, the David Sassoon Library, the Army & Navy Building and of course, the Watson Hotel—all so strongly Victorian that you may be forgiven for thinking you are in London.

Restored over the past decade, these buildings were once the heartbeat of posh colonial life. The Elphinstone College was

Elphinstone College (left), David Sassoon Library and Reading Room (right).

completed in 1888, and claims well-known personalities such as scientist Homi. J. Bhabha, industrialist Jamshedji Tata and political stalwart Pherozeshah Mehta amongst its alumni. Built from a grant by Sir Cowasji Jehangir whose medallion it sports on its exterior façade, the building is dressed with beautiful stone turrets, well-appointed balconies, archways, exquisite floorings and tiled pyramid ceilings. The college building is one of the finest Victorian structures built in colonial India and in 2004, the college was awarded the UNESCO Asia Pacific Heritage Award for Cultural Heritage Conservation.

The Army & Navy Building (left) stands beside the Esplanade Mansion (right).

Likewise, between 1870 and the 1890s the David Sassoon Library and Reading Room, as well as the Army & Navy Stores Building were constructed with very similar façades from the same yellow malad stone to retain the flow of the skyline. The interiors of David Sassoon Library still holds its old-world charm, beckoning readers to leisure time in its quiet gardens with leather-bound books stocked in antiquated rosewood cabinets. The Army & Navy Stores Building, part of the original British chain and a shopping paradise for the highly exclusive British Burra Sahibs of those times, had fallen into complete disrepair until it regained its retail charm with the opening of a department store in its precincts.

Yet for the history it carries within its walls, the *pièce de résistance* of this stretch has to be the dilapidated, mangled Esplanade Mansion—the erstwhile Watson Hotel located beyond the Army & Navy Building. Would you believe that Mark Twain once sat in its balcony and wrote *Following the Equator*? Or that this crumbling building was the venue for the first screening of the Lumière Brothers' Cinematographe in 1896 (opened only to its white patrons)? India's oldest cast-iron building boasted of 130 rooms, a restaurant, lobby bar and even a ballroom during its heydays. The hotel's emphasis on its "Britishness" was such that the restaurant and ballroom was serviced only by English waitresses, epitomising the ultimate mecca for all things posh, rich and white in the Raj days. Unfortunately, when the spurned Jamshedji Tata, previously refused entry on grounds that he was brown-skinned, built and opened the iconic Hotel Taj Mahal, Watson's death warrant was signed, sealed and delivered!

KHAU GALLIES

You don't need to go too deep into the back alleys of the city to get to one of its Khau Gallies (literally the Glutton Lanes).

There is something special about watching your meal being cooked from scratch as you stand there, insist Khau Galli patrons. The way the vendor's lackey goes furiously at the onions and tomatoes while the cook splats a blob of butter (when given pampered service; it's oil otherwise) on the hot griddle, its smokiness permeating the air, the stirring, frying and seasoning according to your order, and the finishing merry dance of the cook's hand as he finally wraps up a dish and slaps it onto a steel plate. Simply salivating! Top it with a price list that is easy on the purse strings and you have the patron's continued loyalty for years together.

Depending on your location, the Khau Galli menu may vary. One of the oldest ones is along Third Agiary Lane, located in Zaveri Bazaar amidst a clutter of narrow lanes, snarling traffic, pedestrians and stray animals. The 1996 book *Bombay* describes how this Khau Galli evolved to meet the strict vegetarian dietary requirements of Gujarati and Marwari merchants who in the 1920s set up a flourishing bullion market in this area. Today, Zaveri Bazaar continues to be frequented by an assortment of women clients, Gujarati, Marwari, Jain diamond sorters and others employed in the jewellery industry. Therefore, it is primarily vegetarian fare on the menu. Bordering the lanes, vendors cook on push-carts with neatly appointed cooking stoves and stacks of steel jars, woks and steel plates. All day long, frenetic business is conducted over plates of *pav bhaji*, *missal pav*, *chapati* and veggies, hot *jalebis*, *dosas*, *vadas* and according to grapevine, even *bhang* (cannabis)-dotted *papads*!

The Khau Galli at Marine Lines is a 30-year-old setup that receives business from the more well-heeled—employees from the neighbouring Income Tax Office, collegians and other office goers. Once again, the mantra is the same—homestyle cuisine at reasonable prices. It's a shade better off in terms of hygiene and for a modest Rs. 12–25, you can grab a small meal of *puri-bhaji* and *chaat* from vendors like Lalit Bhelwala and down it with one of the 40-odd fruit juices on offer at Hans Raj Mandir. Marine Lines also offers the increasingly popular fast food-like pizzas and burgers. Stall owners say they easily get 200 to 300 customers daily,

LOCATION:
Khau Galli,
Zaveri Bazaar

Khau Galli off
Maharshi Karve
Road, Churchgate

Khau Galli,
Mohammad Ali
Road

ensuring that they will be in business for the next 30 years.

If you are looking for food of a carnivorous kind (read *biryanis*, *bheja masalas*, *kheema parathas* and more), head to the Khau Galli around Bohri Mohalla and Minara Masjid in the Mohammad Ali Road vicinity. This being the Muslim heartland, the best time to go is post-sundown during the month-long festivities of Ramzan but take note, it is amongst the most congested parts of the city.

The food on offer is endless. The aroma of skewered *kababs* being roasted over coal, pan-fried *baida rotis* (egg breads), desserts like crispy *jalebis*, melting *malpuas*, smooth-as-silk *phirnis* (rice puddings) and falooda drinks and sherbets are drooling, to say the least . However, hygiene, in the best of times, is a non-starter here. The food is hot off the coals, and that hopefully should take care of the bacteria. If this doesn't work, not to worry—the doctors are there to helpfully put you on courses of amoeba and diarrhoea medications!

Khau Galli at Mohammad Ali Road.

KOLIS

In *Bimbakyan* (the Chronicles of Bimb) penned in 1139, Bombay's islands were described as being already populated by fishermen's colonies and temples. Nine centuries later, these indigenous fisherfolk, called Kolis, continue to abound the coast of Bombay.

Interestingly, during these nine centuries, while Ptolemy's Bombay-Heptanesia (as the seven-island cluster was named by the Greek geographer and astronomer) has morphed into the unrecognisable "clawed hand", the Kolis remain as they were many centuries ago, the odd TV set and fibre-glass boat notwithstanding.

Throughout contemporary Mumbai you see signs of the Koli's Mumbai. For starters, the city's official name Mumbai has a Koli connection, taken as it is from Mumba Devi, the patron goddess of Kolis who is venerated in a famous shrine at Kalbadevi. Names of many areas of Mumbai also come from the original Koli names—Colaba was Kolbat, Apollo Bunder was Palva Bunder (the Palva fish used to be found near this harbour), Machchagaun the original name for Mazagaon, and the list goes on.

Thus in its truest sense, Mumbai belongs to the Kolis, the island's oldest inhabitants. In an irony of sorts, the intervention of India's topmost judiciary was required in the 1960s to prevent rapacious builders from edging out the Kolis from their own land. As such, Koliwadas (Koli villages) like Backbay Reclamation, Worli, Mazagaon, Mahim, Versova and Khar-Danda can still be found dotting the Mumbai coastline. Difficult to miss, these Koliwadas

Koli fishermen preparing their nets for the next catch. can be sniffed from a distance. The smell of the sea and the presence of colourful boats aside, the unsavoury assault of racks of Bombay Duck, pinkish-silver *bombil* fish and salted prawns sun-drying ensure their introduction to every passing visitor!

On the early morning trains, at bus stops and wet markets, you cannot miss the Kolis. Koli women dressed in their traditional *lungat* (sari), *choli* (blouse), green bangles, big red vermillion *bindi* and innumerable gold ornaments make their way to the markets armed with water-dripping wicker baskets full of the day's fresh catch. Notoriously garrulous, argumentative, aggressive and often scandalously abusive, Koli women are a fiercely independent lot, managing the purse-strings in their homes.

Theirs is a clear-cut demarcation of responsibilities. The Koli male, often found lounging in his *surkha* (loin cloth) waist coast and *topi* (cap), is the provider. Boat and net repairs as well as deep-sea fishing are his responsibilities. Koli fishermen are gone for days on, as far out as Goa before returning with the catch of lobsters, clams, *bangda*, *bombil*, pomfret and others. Kolins, the female Koli counterparts, manage almost everything else. They are the ones who get to the docks pre-dawn, negotiate and haggle to get the best-priced catch and then sell it at the wet market. Along with home chores, you'll also find the Kolins sorting, seasoning and drying fish in addition to mending nets and fishing baskets.

According to the 2005 Marine Fisheries Census there are 50,075 Kolis in the city. Speaking either Marathi or Konkani, a dialect of Maharashtra, Kolis are ethnically Marathi Hindu or Christian converts. Amongst the Hindu Kolis there are several sub-castes, and occupationally they are divided into the Dolkars, the ones who fish; and the States, those that trade in the catch. After the monsoon season hiatus during which fishing is suspended, Kolis celebrate their biggest festival, the Narieli Poornima, to mark the return of the fishing season by taking blessings of the sea goddess with offerings of coconuts, milk and incense sticks, irrespective of their religious leanings.

The Koli existence is in serious jeopardy today. Contemporary Mumbai's unheeded construction and pollution is fast eroding the local fish population, endangering not only the environment, but also the people it supports. But the Kolis have been here long before anybody else came on the Heptanesia shores, and aren't about to jump ship anytime soon.

KRISHNA JANMASHTAMI

It has all the elements of a Bollywood flick—young strapping men, dance and music, drama, suspense, thrills and good purpose. Amid singing and dancing, groups of young men form eight to nine-storey high human pyramids to reach and break *handis* (terracotta urns) hung at great heights.

Widely featured in travel magazines and on television programmes, this uniquely Mumbai Janmashtami ritual shows best the zest for life that Mumbaikars pride themselves for. Another of Maharashtrian freedom fighter Bal Gangadhar Tilak's inspired Sarvajanik celebrations (Ganeshotsav being the other one), the Dahi Handi ritual celebrated traditionally by the working classes in this Mumbai manner is like a Bollywoodisque salaam to Hindu mythology. Bollywood in fact has done its own bit in making this festival popular. The song *Govinda Ala Re* (Here Comes The Govinda) from a 1950s Bollywood movie depicting the Dahi Handi ritual has for the longest time been Mumbai's anthem for Janmashtami.

Performed over one late afternoon across every nook and cranny of the city, this spectacle is a re-enactment of young Krishna's (the Hindu deity) pranks. Folklore abound with tales of Krishna's weakness for yoghurt and butter for which he, along with his gang of mischievous friends, would sneak into people's homes and steal butter from *handis* hung from the ceilings.

This ritual takes place a day after the Hindu festival of Krishna Janmashtami which, literally translated, is Krishna's birthday on the eighth day of the month. Hindus believe Vishnu was reincarnated as Krishna (thus regarded as Lord Vishnu's eighth avatar) to mitigate the woes of people tormented by the barbarian King Kansa. Observed on the eighth day of the dark half (Krishna *paksha*) of the month of *Shravan* in the Hindu lunar calendar, Janmashtami falls in August or September.

After celebrating Krishna's birth the previous night, Mumbai wakes up the following morning to its mundane, mid-monsoon routine. But by late afternoon, a buzz picks up and for the next few frenzied hours the city comes to a standstill.

Old, traditional parts of Mumbai like Lalbaugh, Mazagaon, Girgaum and Thane are the best places to catch a glimpse of the festive spirit. *Dahi handis* filled with a mixture of butter, milk and

Crowds cheer as human pyramids form to break the *handis*.

dry fruits are hung at extremely great heights across buildings' balconies, over the streets and even from construction cranes. Public address systems blare songs celebrating Krishna; crowds collect and cries of *"Govinda ala re!"* ring in the air as truckloads of men called Govinda Pathaks (troupes of Lord Krishna) arrive to break the *handis*. A couple of false starts notwithstanding, well-rehearsed *govindas* manage very tall, sometimes 40-ft high human pyramids by adroitly climbing on each other to break the *handis*. As the pyramids are formed, people standing on the higher floors throw water and *gulal* (ceremonial powder), making the whole process a bit more exhilarating.

Of course, all these acrobatics are not just for the thrill or the mushy goodies that spill out from the *handis*. Every time a *handi* is broken, prize money (given out by political parties and sundry community groups) is distributed, at times as attractive a sum as Rs.1 lakh for a *handi*!

Govinda Pathaks forming a human pyramid.

LATA MANGESHKAR

Dubbed the Nightingale of India, Bollywood's most enduring female voice is 78-year-old Lata Mangeshkar, one of Mumbai's most celebrated resident Maharashtrians. With a matchless musical oeuvre in the Indian film industry, she has been the voice behind Bollywood heroines down the decades, from Nargis in the 1940s to Kareena in the 2000s.

Lata Mangeshkar's life story, like most of the dream city's rags-to-riches stories, is about talent, spark and the beauty of Mumbai where, to borrow a rather clichéd expression, nuggets are picked, polished and morphed into sparkling diamonds. Born 28 September 1929, this eldest among four children of a classical singer and theatre actor had to seek a living in the Bollywood studios when she was just 13 after her father passed away and the role of breadwinner fell upon her. With her sister Asha Bhosle, Lata travelled around by local train from the one-room tenement they lived in, doing cameo acting parts in movies to patch through financial distress.

A fortuitous meeting with music director Gulam Haider in 1948 changed Lata Mangeshkar's life. Struggling back in the days when female leads sang with heavier, nasal voices, Lata had been dismissed by Subodh Mukherjee, then the owner of Filmistan Studios, for having a voice too "squeaky". Unperturbed by her so-called thin voice, Gulam Haider wrestled a song for her in the movie *Majboor*. After 32 gruelling takes, the young timid singer was given the green signal. The song was a success and Lata was on a roll.

Life wasn't all glam for the 19-year-old though. Songs were recorded with live orchestras, which meant fortnight-long rehearsals, innumerable retakes and constant moving from studio to studio. Yet not much fazed her. Despite her Marathi-speaking background and non-existent formal education (she had attended only one day of school), Lata acquired an impeccable command of Hindi and Urdu, languages used in Bollywood lyrics. She took Urdu lessons and spruced up her Urdu diction after being ribbed by stylish Pathan hero Dilip Kumar for sounding very colloquial. "These people from Maharashtra sing Hindi and Urdu with an accent that stinks of gravy and rice," he had said.

In 1962, during the post India-China war debacle, her rendition of Kavi Pradeep's non-film, patriotic number *Aye Mere Watan Ke Logon* was so heart-wrenching that Prime Minister Jawaharlal

Lata Mangeshkar, the beloved Nightingale of India.

Nehru and the rest of India were moved to tears. This unforgettable musical composition has since been counted amongst the most well-loved patriotic songs in India.

In a cinematic genre where emotions and storylines are expressed and moved forward via poetry set to music lip-synced on screen by actors, Lata's voice represents the evolution of popular Bollywood music down the past eight decades. Over this span of time, Lata Mangeshkar has sung more than 25,000 songs in 20 languages! She is the 2001 recipient of the Bharat Ratna (India's highest civilian honour), the only other woman to receive it. She was also presented the Dada Saheb Phalke award, and won four Best Playback Singer Awards until she opted out of the race to give younger talent a chance. Lata has not only acted and sung on celluloid; she also composed the musical scores for a couple of movies.

What places this grand dame apart from the rest is obviously her voice timbre and persona. Diminutive, portly, dressed always in a white sari and her trademark diamonds, her thin three-octave-ranged voice comes across as silken-smooth high. Songs rendered by the singer are a delight to the ears not only for her voice, but also for the precision of diction and the gamut of emotions it conveys without much of a fuss. Classical singer Ustad Ameer Khan once commented that what took classical musicians three-and-a-half hours to accomplish, she could do in a couple of minutes.

Lata Mangeshkar continues to live in Bombay's Peddar Road where she first bought an apartment many decades ago. Almost in semi-retirement, the singer loves to take photographs, design diamond jewellery, watch cricket and supervise work in the Deenanath Mangeshkar Hospital she had opened in Pune in memory of her father. In September 2007, Lata Mangeshkar released a new, non-film album of ghazal-like compositions. When asked how and why a new album materialised, she simply replied, "Music is my life. As long as I am, so will my music be."

MANGO MANIA

The fragrant yellow meat can be juiced, diced, cubed, pulped, puréed or simply sucked out of its thin reddish-yellow, translucent jacket. As long as it's a mango, Mumbaikars will clean it off whichever way they can. From grown hefty men to children in their diapers, all seem to go drool-drip and wobbly-kneed at the sight of the Mighty Mangoes.

India produces some 25 varieties of mangoes, but the crown for the most luscious, full-bodied and moist specimen goes to the Alphonso mangoes, or Hapoos as locals call it, that grow during a very short summer season in Maharashtra and the neighbouring state of Gujarat. With the first stern, sweep of summer, when fruit vendors start showcasing these prime beauties, mayhem breaks out in every Mumbai kitchen, café, juice centre and restaurant.

Interestingly, the Portuguese connection of the Alphonso comes from Afonso De Albuquerque, a Portuguese fidalgo who was famous for the packages of mangoes he carried on his trips to Goa. The Konkani locals in Goa named the fruit Aphoos after the fidalgo. With time though, the word Alphonso got corrupted into the much-desired Hapoos!

Crates of Alphonsos beckon mango-loving Mumbaikars at the market.

MANI BHAVAN

LOCATION:

Mani Bhavan
Gandhi
Sangrahalaya:
19 Laburnum Road,
Gamdevi, 400007
Tel: 23805864
Working hours are
9:30 am–6 pm
everyday.
Library open on
all weekdays from
9:30 am–6 pm.
Closed on second
and fourth
Saturdays, and
public holidays.

You needn't be a Gandhian to appreciate this place. For the personal glimpses it offers from Mahatma Gandhi's interactions with world leaders and also the special moments from the Indian freedom struggle, Mani Bhavan is a must-see on every visitor's list. Like the man himself, this place exudes a simplicity which, amidst Mumbai's dazzle, comes as a welcome change.

Mani Bhavan was owned originally by Gandhi's friend, Shri Revashankar Jagjeevan Jhaveri. The plain, three-storey brown bungalow sits on a quiet, tree-lined avenue in Gamdevi, one of Mumbai's old residential areas.

During the 17 years between 1917 and 1934, the Mani Bhavan terrace was a big newsmaker. It was from here that Gandhi launched all the major freedom struggle strategies—civil disobedience, the Salt Satyagraha, Swadeshi, Khadi and the Khilafat movements—which eventually set the sun on the British rule in India. This bungalow was also the venue of Gandhiji's historic arrest on 4 January 1932.

Gandhi's abode
resting serenely at
Laburnum Road.

As you walk in through the narrow, inconspicuous corridor on the ground floor you'll find yourself in a weary library stocked

with books in old wood and glass-panelled cabinets. The floor is tiled and on the walls are mounted black plaques with many oft-heard Gandhiji's quotes.

If you catch yourself asking what you are doing in this fuddy-duddy place, take a harder look at the book cases. It is said that much about a man is explained by his books, and Mani Bhavan's library is a revelation on Gandhiji's voracious appetite for reading. Not surprisingly, world religion and political philosophies seem to have been his favourites.

What really breathes life into this bungalow is a room on the second floor in which Gandhi spent a lot of time spinning the *charkha* (spinning wheel) and receiving prominent congressmen during those years of heavy political turmoil. Cordoned off by a glass panel, the mosaiced white room has been left much as it used to be during Gandhiji's day—sparse, clean, with mattresses on the floor and Gandhiji's slippers, writing desk and *charkha*.

Once out of this section, you will find yourself in the picture gallery where behind glass cabinets, yellowed, framed correspondences—typed and sometimes handwritten—between

Gandhi and Leo Tolstoy, Adolf Hitler, Franklin Roosevelt and many others are displayed. That Gandhi was so intimate with Tolstoy and so acerbic and frustrated with Hitler is a fascinating insight. Photographs and obituaries written following Gandhi's assassination are also displayed here, the most famous one by Albert Einstein who penned, "Generations to come will scarce believe that such a one as this, ever in the flesh and blood, walked up on this earth."

There is also an auditorium where films and speech tapes of Gandhi are screened from time to time, and another room where 28 dioramas depict the life and times of Gandhi. Not to miss as you climb up to the second storey is an old framed poster charting the evolution of the Indian Tricolor.

Mani Bhavan sees a huge number of local school children and foreign visitors daily. After each tour, you will often see **The room where** visitors quietly walking out of the bungalow overwhelmed **Gandhi met all the** and spellbound, almost as if they just had a personal audience **leaders, preserved** with the Mahatma himself. You know then that this is no **as it was.** ordinary museum.

MILLS TO **MALLS**

In post-liberalization India, McTikki Burgers and the hukka-in-a-lounge evenings are cool but cooler still, according to Mumbai's affluent young, is trawling the 15 or more shopping malls dotting the city.

These latest Western fads with names as fancy as InOrbit, Phoenix and Atria have become the favourite poster icons of new India. Often you will hear the affluent talk of awesome family outings, which means a day spent hanging out in the mall's swanky environs, shopping for top Indian and international brands, going to movie multiplexes, discothèques, bowling alleys and a zillion niche restaurants catering to international cuisine.

Yet if you were probe to how space has been created for so many malls amid the clutter of Mumbai, an uncomfortable reality comes forward, visible often in the mall's skyline—a painted chimneystack or shed! Many of these malls have actually come up on land that until two or three decades ago housed textile mills and port establishments that provided livelihoods to a large segment of Mumbai's working class. In fact, Mumbai was called the Manchester of the East because, along with Ahmedabad, it was home to India's textile mills.

The Bombay Spinning Mill was the first mill on Bombay's soil, set up in 1854 by Cowasji Nanabhai Davar. Its success spawned an industry which, fuelled by the American War of Independence and subsequently World War I, established Bombay as an efficient and successful textile producer.

In Girangaon (literally, a village of mills), an area covering 600 acres across Bombay, there were as many as 54 textile mills where cloth was spun, woven, printed and dyed. Serviced by a largely-Marathi rural workforce of close to 250,000 people, the mill workers, some alone and others with families, populated one-room tenements in chawls located in and around the mill areas.

Historian Rajnarayan Chandavarkar wrote in a preface for the book *One Hundred Years, One Hundred Voices; The Millworkers of Girangaon*: "Each mill employed hundreds of workers, mostly from the Konkan region but also from other parts of India. They were Hindu and Muslim, Dalit and other castes...the 1911 census noted that 69 per cent of the population of the city lived in

The Phoenix mill compound, now converted into a mall.

one-room tenements. Bombay of those days was predominantly working class."

As times changed, power looms were introduced in the 1970s. Subsequently in 1982, Bombay mill workers went on an 18-month strike, which sounded the death knell of the mills. One by one, the mills' trademark chimneystacks became cold and bugles quietened. Given that land was a precious asset, defunct mills naturally became prime targets for redevelopment.

Thus, malls appeared. Many of Mumbai's poshest malls have come up in suburbs like Malad and Goregaon. Fuelled not only by the availability of greater space, but also perhaps by the realisation of the suburbanites' need to claim their own place under the affluent sun, these malls especially have been a huge success.

Why malls are mesmerising Indians is probably best explained by looking at what they are replacing. Indians have traditionally shopped at markets which housed generic stores and small boutiques run by "uncles" and "aunties" who'd known your mum and her mum, called you by your first name and offered you the ubiquitous cold drink or *chai* when you walked in. In contrast to this all-too-familiar banality came the glass and steel structures manned by uniformed ushers and sales staff who pepper their conversations with the tad impersonal yet formal "Sir" and "Thank you maam". Snobbish you might say, but it is a charmer! In fact, Mumbai's first mall, Crossroads, initially gained notoriety because the doorman would only allow entry to those who could show a mobile phone or credit card, presumed signs of affluence then! Yet the people simply loved it.

The megapolis is set to see 25 more malls open up shortly as government authorities have released more land for commercial development. At another old, forgotten site where workers once worked the looms, expect the emergence of trendy divas and their chauffeur-driven Hyundais. New economy, new money, new sources of bread and butter! Why not?

MONEY TALKS

LOCATION:

Bombay Stock
Exchange Limited:
Phiroze Jeejeebhoy
Towers, Dalal Street,
Mumbai 400023
Tel: 2721233 / 4

Reserve Bank
of India:
Fort, Mumbai
400001

India Government
Mint, Mumbai:
Shahid Bhagat
Singh Road, Fort,
Mumbai 400023
Tel: 2661735
Nearest stations:
Churchgate and VT

Delhi may be the political hotseat of India, but many would argue that the "Mumbai Moneymeter" rules the nation. The presence of the "Moneybag trio"—the Stock Exchange, Reserve Bank of India and the Mint lends the city the status over trade and commerce which it exercises brazenly over India.

The most important of the trio is the Bombay Stock Exchange (BSE). Mumbai ranks as Asia's largest stock exchange after Tokyo and the fifth largest exchange in the world. More than 4,800 companies are listed on its bourse with a combined market capitalisation of over $ 1.1 trillion, and an average daily turnover of over $ 1.15 billion. Such is its control over contemporary India that even a minor tremor within its walls would send major tremblers throughout the political and economic foundations of the country.

Curiously though, the Phiroze Jeejeebhoy Towers where all the hustling and trading transpires is located not in posh Manhattan-like environs, but in a congested two-car lane called Dalal Street tucked deep in the Fort area. Until 1995, the floors of this stock exchange had reverberated with garrulous out-shouting amongst the pen-and-paper armed brokers. Today the stock exchange has a new vibe. The 28-storey, nondescript building is technologically wired with an electronic system named BOLT, or the BSE Online Trading.

BSE brokers have a vibrant history dating as far back as the 1850s. Stock folklore talks about a motley bunch of 22 *dhoti*-clad, predominantly Gujarati and Marwari brokers who invested a princely sum of Rs. 1 each and began trading among themselves under a tree in the Horniman Circle area outside the former Town Hall. They called themselves The Native Share and Stockbrokers Association. In 1875 it was restructured and formally launched as the BSE, but only in 1928 did the BSE move into its permanent home on Dalal Street. In 1980, at the behest of the BSE Chairman Phiroze Jeejeebhoy, its new multi-storey premises were opened at Dalal Street.

While the stock exchange has often acted as a catalyst in raising many a blood pressure, it is the Reserve Bank of India (RBI) that has kept the tab on the economic pulse. Bombay is where banking first started in India when the General Bank of India was

established in 1786. The bank did not last long, but Bombay's economic importance was on its ascendancy, spurred by the growing shipping and cotton-related businesses. Gradually, the area in the Fort district transformed into a financial hub, with broking agencies, banks and shipping companies setting up shop here.

The RBI was established in 1935 under the recommendations of the Hilton Young Commission and located on Mint Road. Originally housed in what used to be the Imperial Bank of India, RBI got its own majestic building in 1939. In the book *Bombay: The cities within*, the RBI building is described as "utilitarian, giving the impression of security and solidity". The building sports embellishments of two giant 60-ft-high Corinthian columns flanking the main entrance, and the RBI logo above the grilled doorway. With the inauguration of RBI, the country's banking industry began to acquire a cohesive entity. After India's independence in 1949, the RBI, a shareholder's bank till then, was nationalized and became a government-owned institution. Today the RBI is the central bank of the country and also the highest monetary regulatory authority in India.

Yet, long before RBI consolidated Mumbai's credibility as the banking capital, one of the India Government Mints had already been established here in this city, right across from where the RBI building eventually came up. Established in 1829 by the Governor of the Bombay Presidency, the Mint had in its past (1918–1919) even worked as a branch of the Royal Mint of London.

In its post-independence avatar, the Mint continues to be involved in coinage production, gold refining and the production and supply of Working Standards of metric weights, capacity, and linear measures throughout India.

During the infamous coordinated Bombay bombings in 1993, Dalal Street was severely impacted. A car bomb exploded in the basement of the BSE building, and the ensuing carnage killed 50 people at this site alone.

Much was said about this being an attempt to crush the economic spirit. Yet Mumbai is not called the Maximum City for no small reason, as both the stock market and the city bounced back in no time.

The innocuous building of "Mumbai's Moneymeter", the Mumbai Stock Exchange.

MOUNT MARY CHURCH

Are you childless? Plagued by problems in the stomach or your spine? Or is your desired home not materialising? Despair not. Pick up a candle that represents your problems—a wax stomach, spine or house—and light it in the Mount Mary Church. The Virgin Mother will never disappoint.

LOCATION:
Mount Mary Road,
Bandra West

Such is the belief in her miraculous powers that even though Mumbai has been run over by unscrupulous builders, a little hillock in Bandra remains untouched, thanks largely to this 300-year-old church that welcomes lakhs of devotees seeking blessings of the Virgin Mary.

As you make your way up the Mount Mary vicinity you could be misled into thinking you are in an old Portuguese-Christian neighbourhood. Remnants of the distant past when Bandra was essentially a five-village, largely Christian cluster are all over the place—the several stone and wooden crosses, some over a century old, standing outside old tiled homes and road junctions amidst the warren of high-rise buildings.

Marathi residents refer to the church as Mauli Mary, and have nicknamed Mount Mary Hill as Maulicha Dongar (Hill of the Mother). Venerated deeply by people of all faiths, Mauli Mary is also known as the Basilica of Our Lady of the Mount; or simply as Mount Mary to the Bandraites. For Marian devotees especially, the church ranks amongst the most popular Catholic pilgrim destinations in the world. In fact, Pope Pius XII had granted the shrine the status of a "Minor Basilica" in 1954.

The church, built in 1640, has a rather chequered history. It began when Portuguese Jesuit priests brought in an ornamental wooden statue of Virgin Mary with infant Jesus in her arms, and constructed the Nossa Senhora de Monte Chapel on top of a lone hillock. In 1700, avaricious Arab pirates severed a hand of the statue while attempting to rob it of an embellishment and the desecrated statue was removed. A subsequent fire during a Marathi raid in 1738 saw the church gutted. After reconstruction in 1760, the restored Virgin Mother statue was installed once more in the church. In 1904, the current structure, 110-ft long and 38-ft wide with white marble steps on its side, was built.

For a week every year, Bandra springs to life to celebrate the birthday of Virgin Mary. From 9 to 15 September, after a Novena of morning and evening prayers in the Basilica, Bandra celebrates the Mount Mary Fair. During this week, all normal life and roads going towards Mount Mary virtually come to a standstill. The road leading to the top of the hillock is dressed with banners, lights and makeshift stalls selling votives, candies, sweetmeats, shoes, clothes, sundries, sticky Goan desserts and most important of all, candles and wax figurines or *baulis*.

Queer yellow, blue and pink "body-part candles" and other miniature wax figurines are what the vendors call *baulis* (literally dolls in Konkani, the Goan dialect). Lying stacked in wicker baskets or hung from metal screws, these are the offerings for the Mother. Inside the church and below the altar are metal stands where devotees place lighted candles representing the afflicted body part or their wishes. The belief is that such prayers would move Mauli Mary to miraculously bring wellness and fulfilment of all wishes. Drawn by that hope, every year Mumbai embraces the Mother's birthday just as gladly as it later welcomes Ganapati Bappa to its homes in the same season.

Exterior façade of Mount Mary Church.

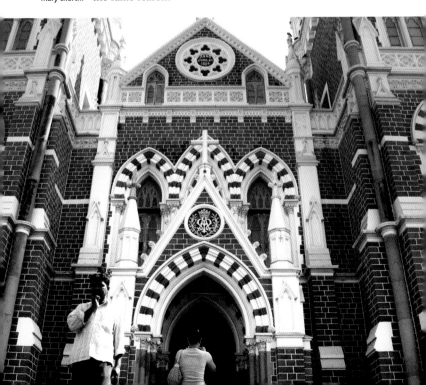

MUMBA DEVI **TEMPLE**

A long time ago, a giant called Mumbarak romped the islands of Bombay. After receiving a blessing from Lord Brahma (the Creator; part of the Hindu trinity of the Creator, Preserver and Destroyer) that assured him invincibility, Mumbarak wrecked havoc on the inhabitants of the islands. Traumatised, the hapless people beseeched the gods for help. Lords Vishnu and Shiva (the other parts of the Hindu trinity) fashioned an eight-armed goddess, a Devi, who fought with the giant and brought him down on his knees. As an act of repentance Mumbarak implored to be allowed to combine his name with that of the goddess, and also pledged to build a temple. That, as the legend explains, was the genesis of the Mumba Devi temple.

> **LOCATION:**
> Bhuleshwar
> Best reached by local bus or a taxi.
> Open on all days except Monday.

Located in the famed Bhuleshwar-Kalbadevi area, one of the city's crazily gridlocked places, Mumba Devi is the temple which gave Bombay its original name, Mumbai. The word Mumba is a Sanskrit derivative, the original being Maha Amba (a name for the Hindu goddess of Shakti), to which *'ai'* (mother in Marathi) was added on—therefore forming Mumbai.

Mumba Devi, essentially a representation of the goddess of Shakti (strength and power), is the patron goddess of the native Kolis and the *agris* (the salt collectors). Its temple was originally built by the Kolis at Phansi Talao adjacent to the VT Station. Somewhere between 1737 and 1766, after the East India Company decided to expand the precincts of the Fort area, the temple was demolished. A generous largesse from Pandurang Shivaji Sonar, a goldsmith, saw the reconstruction of the temple at its present location. That was followed in 1830 with the construction of the Mumbadevi Tank.

As the city's patron deity, Mumba Devi sees a large number of the city's residents. Vendors, traders and small business families make a dignified living out of the sale of offerings for the goddess such as coconuts, sweets, flowers and miniature adornments in the lanes leading to the temple.

A visit to the Mumba Devi temple is not so much for its architectural perspective but for a pure spiritual experience. Despite being in the heart of South Mumbai, the temple, quite like Banganga at Walkeshwar, transports you to some quaint temple town like Varanasi where the business of connecting with the gods seems to become the business of living.

At the temple, the goddess is represented by a stone statue that sits under a silver-studded wooden canopy, dressed in a trademark silver crown, nose-stud and gold necklace. A stone idol of Annapurna—the goddess of food and fertility and another avatar of Shakti—sits on her stone peacock to Mumba Devi's left. In front of Mumba Devi stands a copper statue of a tiger which dates back to 1890 when it was donated by a pearl merchant. The temple also houses shrines of other deities—Ganesh, Maruti, Mahadev, Indrayani, Murlidhar, Jagannath, Narsoba and Balaji.

If you look closely at the statues there, you will notice a distinct pattern: their faces have eyes, noses and other features, but where their mouths should be, a large gaping hole with red vermillion is applied there. Unique to the Mumba Devi temple, this apparently is symbolic of Mumba Devi being Mother Earth.

In the best of times the Bhuleshwar-Kalbadevi areas are not for the faint-hearted tourists, and access by taxi is recommended. Be prepared: Tuesdays, being the day for special prayers to the goddess, will prove a bit more challenging for visits.

A sight also not to be missed is the *chapatti* makers in the lane down from Mumba Devi temple. Out in the alley, under a tarpaulin shelter sits an assembly line of 10 to 15 men, some kneading dough, others rolling out the *chapatti* and still another batch cooking and stacking them. Rather surreal! It transpires that these are orders for small food joints.

Worshippers buying flowers at the Mumba Devi Temple compound.

MUMBAI'S BAZAAR MANIA

What Chatuchak in Bangkok and Kowloon's Ladies Market do to a shopper' sensibilities, Mumbai's Chor Bazaar and Fashion Street do just as well. From period furniture and antique reproductions to Guess summer line knockoffs and accessories for that diva look, all needs are best fulfilled in its innumerable alleys.

Chor Bazaar (literally translated as the thieves' market) is a thriving antique flea market that has dressed many a Bollywood period flick with furniture, lamps and sundry bric-a-brac. Open Saturdays to Thursdays, it is located in the heart of the congested Muslim district of Mohammad Ali Road and is best accessed by taxi.

The market's origins are unclear. Rumour has it that it sprung up during the World War depression when, desperately in need of money, families reached out to these lanes to hawk their personal heirlooms. Nevertheless, its name is credited to a notorious episode dating back to the 1920s when a violin belonging to Queen Victoria was stolen from her ship as it berthed in Bombay and was soon traced to this market!

War memorabilia, old 48 rpm music records, film posters, antique *gara saree* borders, temple and church carvings, ethnic furniture, and sculptures and statuettes from a long-gone era—some original and others fake or clever reproductions—vie for your attention as you walk through the bylanes starting from Mutton Street off Mohammad Ali Road.

Trusting your instincts alone in spotting an original in that pandemonium requires a great measure of luck and exceptionally keen eyes. More often than not, the real stuff is tucked at the back of the shops, so browse around, and bargain heavy. If the budget does not allow for the original, try the reproductions—they aren't a bad buy; the finesse used in giving the weather-beaten look could well cheat a layperson's eyes!

In a parallel of sorts, with the same degree of authenticity and style is Fashion Street—a young fashionista's garment manna. Sitting in Mulund or Prabhadevi, Milan and Paris

LOCATION:

Chor Bazaar:
Mutton Street,
between SV Patel
and Moulana
Shaukat Ali Road,
Mumbai 400003

Fashion Street:
MG Road,
Mumbai 400032

Open from
10 am–7 pm

might be unattainable, but if you have got aspirations for the hot-'n-happening look that scorches the Euro ramp, Fashion Street, popularly abbreviated as FS, may be your answer. A regular haunt for collegians and all of middle-class Mumbai-on-the-go, Fashion Street offers pizzazz on a frayed budget. Clothes here are export rejects and the clothiers, or rather the modest stall owners, are mainly migrants with little or no fashion sense, though well-compensated with an astute business sense.

Located opposite the Bombay Gymkhana along Azad and Cross Maidan are 130 to 140 illegal stalls that set up shop everyday. Under makeshift plastic awnings stretched out onto the sidewalk, denims, shirts, skirts, leggings, crocheted boleros, children's clothes and the latest Bollywood-inspired knockoffs are displayed on hangers dangling from bamboo poles. Intermittently, there are also shops that sell belts, sandals and shoes. A narrow pathway is left for customers to negotiate their way as they move from stall to stall checking out prices and products. As long as you are happy to compromise on the irregular hem or a missing button on a Guess shirt, Fashion Street will please you no end.

Here too, bargain heavy. All too often, healthy banter can be heard between persistent buyers and the adamant *"bhaiya"* (as these stall owners are referred to), standing on his or her own baseline prices. This is a repeat scenario, but obviously business is good. Why else would the stall owners continue running their operations here for so many decades?

Clothes galore at
Fashion Street.

MUMBAI'S GREEN MANNA

Mumbai breathes because of greens like these. The Sanjay Gandhi National Park and Hanging Gardens are just two of the most celebrated green pockets revered like manna from heaven by Mumbaikars. While one offers natural forested bounty, the other is for those, especially families and kids, wanting a roll in the manicured green, or looking for Mumbai's best vantage point to spot the Queen's Necklace in all its iridescence.

Dating back to fourth century BC, Sanjay Gandhi National Park is located smack in the middle of the northern Mumbai suburbs fringing Film City, Borivli and the Thane district. Within the park precincts are the Yeoor and Nagla Hills and the Tulsi and Vihar lakes. Back in the first century BC, during the

LOCATION:

Sanjay Gandhi
National Park
Nearest station:
Borivli

Hanging Gardens
and Kamla
Nehru Park:
Malabar Hill
Open daily from
5 am–9 pm

Butterflies are one of the many beautiful sights that greet visitors to the Sanjay Gandhi National Park.

Buddhist Mauryan King Ashoka's reign, the park used to receive Buddhist monks who sculpted out caves from the rocky outcrop as shelters. Kanheri Caves, one of the prime examples of those Buddhist caves, is found within the park's precincts.

The 104 sq km of forest cover apparently qualifies Sanjay Gandhi National Park as the largest park in the world located within municipal city limits. It is home to an estimated 800 types of flowering plants like the rare Karvi that blooms once in seven years and envelopes the parks' hill slopes in a purple hue. Also present are 284 kinds of birds, 5,000 species of insects, 150 species of butterflies, the most famous being the endangered and world's largest Atlas Moth; 50 kinds of reptiles as well as 36 types of mammals, including panthers and predatory man-eating leopards!

Sanjay Gandhi National Park is popular amongst its two million visitors yearly for various reasons. People come to see the tiger safari, visit the Kanheri Caves, the Jain and Trimurti temple, all in the park's precincts, and even go for boating in the lakes. This is essentially de rigueur stuff, unless you want to explore more adrenalin-pumping activities that the park offers—trekking, hikes on the Highest Point trail, rappelling, rock climbing and even a bird-spotting annual race called the Mumbai Bird Race!

While nature watchers moan that the park is shrinking even as encroaching illegal shanty town settlements located in the park's precincts become victims to leopards, this park is the only forest cover that counterbalances Mumbai's pollutants-laced air.

In contrast, the Hanging Gardens, in no way similar to its namesake in Babylon, was made way back in 1880. The garden is laid out over three reservoirs processing 30 million gallons of fresh water that is supplied to Mumbai. Its genesis appears to lie in the belief that the garden would prevent the potable water from getting contaminated by the nearby Parsi Tower of Silence, the Parsi burial tower where corpses are left in an open well to be fed off by vultures.

Worthy of a botanist's enquiry, this terraced garden is perched at the top of the western side of Malabar Hill, but is bereft of trees on the tank itself apparently because the soil laid out on the reservoir is only six to 30 inches deep! Hanging Gardens though sports hedges trained and manicured into life-sized animal shapes. Rechristened Ferozeshah Mehta Gardens, it has an adjacent twin called the Kamla Nehru Park, both surprisingly popular destination for families. The park's main attractions are the strange sunny yellow-beaked, penguin-shaped litterbins, a prominent idiosyncratic fixture and a play area complete with a bizarre huge "Old Woman's Shoe" for the kids to play around in.

At Hanging Gardens, any sunny day is a good time to visit. And at the Sanjay Gandhi National Park, November to February

Hedges sculpted to various shapes in the Hanging Gardens. is ideal for birdwatchers, and sunrise or sundown of the peak summer months ideal for animal tracking. To avoid, except for the devout, is a park visit on Shivratri, a one-day Hindu festival when the Shiva temple in the park's precincts receives close to 100,000 devotees.

In an overpopulated city choking on its own filthy water and polluted air, who can grudge these marvels? Sanjay Gandhi National Park and the Hanging Gardens are indeed a must-go for anybody looking for a time-out from the city's craziness.

MUMBAI SUBURBAN RAILWAYS

6:22 slow, 7:56 Virar, 8:02 fast. No, these aren't cryptic clues on the Bombay Stock Exchange index, but a sampler of what time means for the "Mumbai locals", the Bambaiya slang for Mumbai suburban trains.

Quite unlike the rest of the country, the Mumbai locals are mostly dependably punctual, regular, disciplined and efficient. Rather uniquely, they also have separate compartments for ladies. The trains are slotted in categories of fast, which stop only at the bigger stations and are preferred for longer distance travel; and slow, which stop at every station.

Of course, these local trains offer the "unique comfort" of packed, hot, sweaty rides especially during peak hours, but they

Barely any standing room as passengers hang on for their lives. are fast, a key operative in Bambaiya parlance. Although visitors to the city marvel at the Mumbaikar's audacity to test his life and limb to the system that is seemingly imploding, Mumbaikars love their locals.

Accomplishing to enter and exit a rush hour train is considered a baptism to Mumbai. While the worst of the dog-eat-dog spirit is exemplified best by local commuters, there is also a strange sense of camaraderie those years of commuting the same route brings amongst these travellers. Huddled together, passengers shell peas, cut veggies, do *bhajan* (devotional singing) sessions and play cards. The trains have also been the unlikely scene of many a romance flick, which Bollywood has captured on its silver screen poignantly in movies like *Saathiya*.

Ranked Asia's oldest railway system, the first train that ran in India, then under the unified Railways, was on 16 April 1853, covering a distance of 21 km between Bombay and Thane. With bare third-class coaches devoid of seats, no toilets, and windows so far back they could be reached only by the taller commuters, this was called the *bakra gadi* (goat carriage).

In terms of capacity, the story isn't much different today. Ponder these statistics: each day 5,000 passengers travel on each train, as against the stipulated capacity of 1,710. That adds up to roughly 6.1 million commuters taking the train, which is more than half the total passenger traffic of the Indian Railways. The passenger density of the Mumbai locals is highest amongst urban railway systems anywhere in the world, even Tokyo or Seoul.

And here is the macro view: 2,067 suburban trains run every four minutes, covering 302 route kilometres of Mumbai over three corridors of rail lines—the Western Railway line from Churchgate Station to Dhanahu Road, the Central Line from VT Station to Kalyan, and the Harbour line from VT Station again to Panvel.

On 12 July 2006 during the evening rush hour traffic, the suburban train on the western corridor was brought to a halt after eight powerful coordinated bombs detonated on the train, killing 183 people and wounding 600. Mumbaikars were undeterred. They unflinchingly swore by the local trains, calling it their lifeline.

Indeed, Mumbai without its trains would be a city without its heartbeat.

VT Station (Chatrapati Shivaji Terminus)

India's inaugural steam train from Mumbai to Thane was flagged off in 1853 from this very railway station. In 2004, UNESCO nominated it as a World Heritage Site, acknowledging it for its outstanding "19th century railway architecture" as well as the "advanced technical and structural" solutions it offers as a railway station. In contemporary Mumbai, this railway station is the headquarters of the Central Railways, a strategic arm of the Indian railway network.

Called VT (Victoria Terminus, named after the Queen Victoria), swarms of people who first arrive at Mumbai by train every day are greeted by this majestic Gothic edifice. Aptly, this is also their introduction to the city of dreams.

Rechristened in 1996 as Chatrapati Shivaji Terminus (after the famed Maratha King Shivaji), VT Station ranks amongst the world busiest and most beautiful railway stations. After ten years in the making, it was completed in 1888 at a phenomenal cost of Rs. 1.6 million. Its designer and architect Frederick Williams Stevens, who had by then designed many other colonial buildings, cleverly married elements of the Victorian Italianate Gothic Revival architecture and traditional Indian architecture to create an unparalleled colonial masterpiece. It is said that after being signed up for VT Station's construction, Stevens travelled to Europe to study designs of other railway stations. Coincidentally, VT has a marked resemblance to London's Pancras Station.

The station's building stands out from a distance with the statue of Progress, torch in hand, looking down from the top of the ribbed central dome. VT's entrance greets you with sculptured statues of the Lion of Britain and the Tiger of India sitting atop solid pillars flanking the main grilled gates. Straight up on the second floor sits a statue of Queen Victoria, who was then the reigning monarch of the British Empire. The stone frontage is replete with Gothic spires, arches, sculptures of peacocks, gargoyles and other animals flying out of the gables. Equally striking are intricately carved friezes-like GIPPR logos of the GIP Railway Company framed in a stone medallion, busts of railway directors and other men representing 16 Indian castes, and also a much-photographed horizontal panel showing different modes of transports. Connected to the main building

is the 330-ft deep and 1,200-ft long train platform divided into 14 working platforms.

Visitors to VT Station may be overwhelmed by the millions of people being served, but look beyond that. The interiors of the station, designed and decorated by students and professors of J.J. School of Art under Frederick Stevens' supervision merit a good look. Reminiscent of a cathedral, the station has tall columns supporting arched ceilings, grills and railings in ornamental brass and iron, wood carvings, Italian marble tiles and an imposing grand staircase.

The grand Victoria Terminus is a sight to behold. Unarguably, nothing presents a better welcome to the Mumbai megapolis than the colonial magnificence of Chatrapati Shivaji Terminus.

MUSLIMS OF MUMBAI

Islam binds them well and truly. When the Maulvi's *azaan* (call to *namaz* or prayer) goes out, almost everything around Crawford Market and Mohammed Ali Road comes to a standstill to say the *namaz*. This stretch up to Byculla has the largest concentration of the city's Muslim population. Much as they all seem similar to our untrained eye, this area of Mumbai best showcases the eclectic immigrant Muslim populace of the megapolis.

Do not be too surprised if you find Mumbaikars loathe to go there because you do run a risk of slugging it out in notorious traffic jams on Mohammed Ali Road. Once on the J.J. Flyover (named after the J.J. Hospital located in this area) though, one does get moving. Patience is the key.

In this Mumbai, life pans out in a totally different patina. The place has a vibe which almost transports you to a typical Muslim city like Hyderabad. You will hear the *azaan* from neighbouring mosques five times a day, and shops and roads have distinctly Muslim-sounding names. Congested chawls interspersed with beautiful minars of mosques peep over the drab chawl skyline and the sea of humanity makes you wonder: Does all of Mumbai live in this small stretch?

Men and women here sport kohl-lined eyes, and dress codes are strikingly different from what you would see in other parts of the city. Men wear the *Taqiyas* (crocheted prayer cap) and women are dressed in the *burkha* and *hijab* (the cloak and veil, often black and sometimes in sequinned, embroidered light pastels). The air here is often thick with the smell of attar, blended concentrates of floral and wood-based essential oils popularly used as perfume by Muslims. And food rules the marketplace; areas here are identified as much by its people as its restaurants and vendors serving meats, biscuits and sweetmeats cooked in different styles.

If you were to retrace their steps back in time, the oldest Muslims immigrants here would probably have been the Konkani Muslims who came from the coastal areas across Western India. Muslims from Hyderabad, Kerala and the Hindi heartland who formed a large part of Mumbai's porters, weavers, restaurateurs and tailoring workforce came in at later stages.

What makes the city's Muslim populace so colourful are also the immigrants with different lineages and backgrounds. Mumbai has migrants from Shiraz in Iran, who came here as attar sellers and stayed on to continue dominating the city's attar and perfumery businesses. The Iranian mosque in the Dongri area was built by this lot. You will see them sitting behind counters stacked with exquisite glass jars of attars at the Mohammed Ali Road perfumeries, as well as more upmarket shops at Marine Drive's Oberoi Hotel and Colaba Causeway, which at one point was heavily patronised by Mid-Eastern Arab tourists.

Equally well-known are the Memons, though for a different reason. These Sunni Muslim converts from the Hindu Lohana business community of Sindh and Kutch courted much notoriety when the infamous Memon terrorist, Tiger Memon along with his other accomplices, was nailed down for his involvement in the 1994 Bombay terrorist blasts. This apart, Memons are known to be a philanthropic lot and have built many madrasas and masjids, such as the Minara Masjid on Mohammed Ali Road.

It is however the Bohra and Khoja Muslims from Gujarat who are the most fascinating and progressive here in Mumbai. With their keen business sense, urban affluence and lifestyle, as well as non-orthodox customs and traditions, these people are clustered in residential buildings in and around the Bohri Mohalla. This mohalla is famous for the Raudat Tahera mausoleum, built in the Fatimad style of Egypt by the cluster's residents two decades ago.

The Khojas, a small Shiite community of the Ismaili branch of Islam, are distinct in the manner in which they have assimilated Hindu customs and traditions. Bohras, again Gujarati Shias, are well-known both for their involvement in international trade and commerce, as also for a less strict dress code for their women—they wear a *burkha* variant called *ridah*, which comes in pleasant pastel colours like pink, cream and bottle green, and is embellished with delicate floral embroidery, sequins and laces.

Put together, it is this Muslim mosaic that so uniquely describes Mumbai's Muslims, and it is only when you get there that you comprehend why this is regarded as Mumbai's Muslim heartland.

Overleaf:
Thousands of
Mumbai's Muslims
come to prayer
at the mosque
compounds.

NARIMAN POINT

On 12 March 1993, when a series of 13 coordinated bomb explosions brought the megapolis to a halt, it became obvious that the terrorists had chosen to hit Mumbai where it hurt most—the bazaars, the Mumbai Stock Exchange and Nariman Point, corporate India's life breath.

Located at the end of Marine Drive and dubbed "Mumbai Manhattan" because of its tight cluster of more than 40 drab, boxy skyscrapers huddled together on approximately 77 acres of reclaimed land, Nariman Point is the headquarters for most financial services, MNCs, large corporate houses and even the Maharashtra Government's Legislative Assembly, the Vidhan Sabha.

Nariman Point got its name from K.F. Nariman, a Parsi corporator and visionary who in the 1920s, as chronicled in the book *Bombay: The cities within*, had spearheaded public opposition against the black market procurement of imported steel for the backbay reclamation venture, which subsequently was discontinued.

In the 1960 to 1970s the reclamation process was restarted. Again, it was conducted in a haphazard manner, this time with the collusion of the politicians and builders. Despite a seafront and a vantage location, Nariman Point grew into one of the shabbiest and most disorganised business districts, with "no planning for support services like roads, parking, restaurants and green spaces", apparently a victim of political and builder lobby avarice and corruption.

Ironically, despite its almost choked scenario, Nariman Point continues to feature amongst the costliest places for setting up office anywhere in the world. At $138.41 per sq ft per annum, Nariman Point ranks fifth in the list of the world's top ten most expensive office centres, beating metropolises like Paris, New York, Hong Kong and Singapore!

In recent times, heightened by the awareness that Nariman Point is on the verge of collapse with over 300,000 office goers, no infrastructure and unending vehicular traffic snarls, a new sea link has been announced. Once up and running, it is hoped that the 16-km long Worli-Nariman Point sea link project will de-congest the traffic in the area.

Nariman Point, Mumbai's commercial and financial district.

Bandra-Kurla Complex

What Mumbai failed to achieve with Nariman Point, it is hoped it will with the Bandra-Kurla Complex, simply called BKC, the two suburbs, Bandra and Kurla, it flanks into.

The BKC is meant to be modern Mumbai's showcase business district. Builders revel in statements like, "It'll be the second business district, not the secondary district." Imposing glass and steel skyscrapers with office complexes, five-star hotels, a convention centre and an entertainment centre complete with mini golf courses and drive-in theatres are in the making.

The Complex, as Mumbai's auto rickshaw drivers like to call BKC, is already up and running, and has attracted big government and corporate names such as ICICI, Citibank, State Bank of India, IL & FS, Bank of Baroda, Securities Exchange Board of India, Reserve Bank of India , Jet Air, the Nifty (National Stock Exchange) and the Diamond Bourse.

Already quite a success, rental rates here are comparable with Nariman Point. However, unlike only 2.32-million sq ft of space available at Nariman Point, 15 million sq ft of floor space is waiting to get picked up at BKC!

If all goes as envisaged, this business district will be sure to offer competition to Shanghai, a dream all Mumbaiwallahs hope to see fulfilled at some point in their lives!

NATIVE TOWNS

You may run the risk of walking off the known path, but if you haven't experienced this, you have cheated on half of Mumbai.

Plato is famously quoted as saying that a city is what it is because of its citizens. Indeed, the British Raj may have groomed Mumbai as its *pucca* Presidency town, but much of the residential and trading establishments outside the Burra Saheb's Colaba town and Fort area were set up by intrepid, migrant trading communities that were lured into Bombay during the 18th century. The somewhat seamless cluster comprising CP Tank, Bhuleshwar, Kalbadevi, Jhaveri Bazaar, Sheikh Memon Street and Lohar Chawl where these migrants from different states, cultural backgrounds and religious affiliations—Gujarati, Koli, Kamathi, Parsi, Marwari, Bania and Muslim—made homes and business for themselves, is today one of the most densely packed areas of the city.

This is how Native Town used to be as well. Walk with a local through that maze of narrow, meandering lanes and Bombay circa 1800s will stand before you. Brave the nudge and the dodge, and trawl deeper and deeper into that congested claustrophobia. The colours, mesmerising sights, people and architecture changing from cluster to cluster are bound to leave an indelible Mumbai footprint in your mind.

Costume jewellery market for the adornment of deities in Bhuleshwar.

If you want to explore a typical Hindu precinct, you should start in the Bhuleshwar-Kalbadevi cluster. Its roots tracing back to the late 1700s, this area is crammed with Jain deras chawls and crumbling commercial establishments fronting brightly-painted Rajasthani and Gujarati façades, reflecting the communities that inhabit this place. True to its "enterprise city" acronym, single-room shopkeepers, mostly descendants of the original migrants, sit on their *otlas* (raised shop floor) busily hustling a variety of wares—brass, steel, copper and aluminium utensils, traditional adornments for married women, saris, *bindis* and bangles of all sizes, shimmer and shine.

Bhuleshwar is the place to target exquisite silver bric-a-brac at the Chandi Bazaar (silver market) and costume jewellery for women as well as for adornments on statuettes of Hindu deities. For fabric of all kinds, head to Moolji Jetha (cloth market) in Kalbadevi. Over tiny glasses of strongly-brewed tea, sales are made over bales and bales of chiffons, cotton, synthetics, tissues and brocade, often finding their way to many a designer's table.

If all this is too chaotic for comfort, head past the old arched gateway into the leafy, spacious precincts of the Jain Panjarapole, a shelter for sick and aged animals, and you will be in tranquil paradise. Established in 1834 by Seth Motichand Amichand, a wealthy Jain merchant, this shelter houses some 2,000 cows and other animals. The Panjarapole is a highly venerated place for

Earning some brownie points with the gods at the Kalbadevi Panjrapole.

all Hindu and Jain devotees who, as part of their daily religious ritual, come here to feed the cows a staple offering of *gur* (a sugarcane derivative), *chana* (boiled black gram) and fodder. How special the cow is to the Hindus and its religious connotation is beautifully explained in the old framed poster hung on the entrance to the Panjarapole.

The Bhuleshwar-Kalbadevi area is also a temple cluster—five large temples and several smaller ones crowd the bylanes here. It is said that all the 84 major *devtaas* (Hindu deities) reside in this vicinity. Counted amongst Mumbai's most respected temples are the Bhuleshwar Bholenath Mandir, a 150-year-old Shiva temple that gave Bhuleshwar its name; Laxmi Narayan Mandir, with beautiful decorative carvings on its dome and a European-style Vedic school in its precincts; Samudri Mata Mandir, Digambar Jain Mandir and the Mumbadevi Mandir.

Naturally, this area is a major supplier for all things religious. Flowers, offerings and other knick-knacks needed for Hindu prayer ceremonies and weddings are available only in this area. Shops in the 125-year-old Madhavbaug are dedicated statue dealers, working only with statues of deities in marble, clay, terracotta, metal and other materials. It is fascinating to walk

Hindu wedding paraphernalia on sale at Kalbadevi.

into one of these statue shops. Hindu deities big and small sit in cluttered rows on the display shelves almost as if the entire Hindu pantheon has come to life. Flowers, another major component in all Hindu ceremonies, are available in abundance in the next alley with the century-old floral decorators at Phool Galli (flower lane).

A short walk away at Zaveri Bazaar, the scene changes perceptibly. Zaveri Bazaar is Mumbai's biggest jewellery market, and flanking the street are small jewellery and pawn shops where gold, diamond and silver glisten from every shop window. If you want to experiment with some spicy local savouries here, you can check out the Khau Galli in the Third Agiary Lane, renowned for its rows of roadside food vendors. Hygiene standards may be suspect, so be warned!

If you walk further onto Sheikh Memon Street beyond the honking cars, aggressive push-carts and vendors, you will sight a white mosque. It may not be the prettiest in town (especially when compared to Haji Ali Dargah), but Jumma Masjid jettisons you to the fringe of Mumbai's Muslim heartland. Fridays being the day for the holy *namaz* (hence giving the masjid its name), this street is a nightmare to walk on. On

The Jumma Masjid at Sheikh Memon Street.

any other day though, it is a virtual treasure trove for the "house-proud-on-a-budget". Here, the best-priced electronics and plastic household knick-knacks are sold. And despite its Muslim composition, the place co-exists peacefully with the Hindu-dominated Mangaldas Cloth Market and Mirchi Galli, a narrow lane that sells spices of all varieties. A must-visit is the fourth generation-run Vadilal Champaklal & Co., where shelves are stocked with tall clear glass jars of cardamoms, cloves, saffron, nutmeg, cinnamon and spices galore, quite

A colourful splash of spice-inspired mouth fresheners at Mirchi Galli.

in the manner as it was done 60 years ago. Everest Masalas, a household name in branded spices, has its origin from this humble shop floor.

If you yearn for a drink after all that body-contorting, mind-numbing experience, head to Badshah Juice Centre located on the main road across the Crawford Market. One of the best in town, swear the Mumbaiwallahs, this watering hole cranks the health elements, indulging you with its famous falooda milkshakes and fresh fruits juices.

PARSIS

Of Indo-Aryan stock, the physical appearance and demeanour of the Parsis are as distinct from other Bombayites as are chalk and cheese. They are tall, pale-complexioned with a broad forehead and a rather prominent aquiline nose. Harmless but infamous for their idiosyncratically-spoken Gujarati and Hindi, peppered liberally with expletives and a temper to match, Parsis are followers of Zoroastrianism, probably the world's oldest monotheistic religion founded some 3,500 years ago.

LOCATION:
Cusrow Baug,
Colaba Causeway

The forefathers of these immigrant Persians had come to India in the year AD 720 to save their religion from brutal religious persecution. In 1736, at the invitation of the British, a Gujarat-based Parsi shipbuilder named Lowji Nusserwanji Wadia arrived in Bombay with ten of his carpenters to build the Bombay Shipyard. The rest is Parsi history, intertwined intimately with the history of contemporary India, and more specifically, contemporary Mumbai which the majority call home.

Today, all kinds of industries, from aviation to car manufacturing, steel, hospitality and media, carry a Parsi imprint. Names of roads and buildings, statues in the parks and many of India's big industrial giants almost always reveal a Parsi benefactor or initiator—Jamshetji Nusserwanji Tata, scientist Homi Bhabha, Dadabhai Naoroji, the Parsi Congress Nationalist, Madame Cama the freedom fighter, industrialist and Indian Airlines pioneer JRD Tata, music conductor Zubin Mehta, Fardoonji Marzban's *Bombay Samachar* (the oldest continuously published paper in India), Godrej Industries, the Readymoney and Wadia families…the list goes on.

Ask the Mumbaikars to describe the Bawaji, the colloquial term for Parsis, and they may brand them as wackos! Pose the same question to the Bawajis though and they may tell you that they are beyond comparison—educated, successful and yes, superior.

Ironically, Parsis nurse a "Burra Sahib hangover". Parsi enclaves like Cusrow Baug in Colaba—the *crème-de-la-crème* Parsi cluster located within screaming distance of the cacophonous Colaba Causeway, serve as a perfect example. Beyond the humongous

An *agiary* inside
Cusrow Baug , a
Parsi enclave.

gates of the idyllic Cusrow Baug, Parsi gentry in their evening best sit in the pavilion (their club house) playing rummy over a drink and a smoke while speaking the most clipped Queen's English. Children play in the manicured gardens and young adults rough it out at the soccer field. And for all things spiritual, the Baug has its own fire temple, consecrated in 1935—a tranquil space where Parsi men in their skull caps and women in their saris and dresses with scarf-covered heads come to pray to Zarathustra.

Uncomfortably mystical and somewhat suspicious to non-Parsis though is the Parsis' religious exclusiveness and their practices. Mumbai may be home to around 43 Parsi *agiaries*, yet all save one are out of bounds to non-Parsis. Deserving special mention is this aberration—the Bhika Behram Well, located at the junction of Karamveer Bhaurao Patil Marg and Cross

Maidan. As it is a sweet water well in an area with brackish sea water, this Zoroastrian shrine built in 1725 by Behram, a Gujarati Parsi traveller, is open to non-Parsis.

In the Zoorastrian faith, fire and water are considered the purest elements and fire is a medium to connect with God, called Ahura Mazda. Intriguing are their Towers of Silence called Dakhmas, a place where the Parsis practise a rather controversial burial tradition. One of these is located in South Mumbai's Malabar Hill. Housed within would be an open cylindrical stone structure on which Parsi corpses are left for resident vultures to devour the body. The belief is that this practice prevents defiling natural elements like earth, fire and water. Quirky no doubt!

Affluence and intellect notwithstanding, tremendous weightage is placed on racial purity, resulting in the Parsis becoming a dying community. Tightly controlled by the Parsi Panchayat, a powerful and cash-rich governing body that sits judgment on all contentious religious, social and charitable issues, even proselytizing, conversions and inter-faith marriages are unacceptable. Children born into a mixed marriage where a Parsi girl marries outside her community are not considered Parsi. Today, fewer than 70,000 Parsis are left in India, and an equal number is scattered around the globe. The Parsis are further plagued by an extremely low birth rate, with just seven births per 1,000 individuals.

A group of Parsi men congregate for a leisurely afternoon.

Soon, the Parsis must decide what matters more to them—a Parsi community or racial purity. For the Bombayites though, the Parsi presence will live till time immemorial in the various landmarks across the city.

PRINCE OF WALES MUSEUM

The colonisers definitely had a thing for museums. Just as it was in England, Mumbai was also the recipient of museums, the most impressive being the Chatrapati Shivaji Maharaj Vastu Sangrahalaya, listed as one of the 60 best museums in the world.

This museum was simply known as the Prince of Wales Museum during pre-Independence days. If you have come to know the Bombay (or rather, Mumbai) scene better by now, you would have noticed how the resurgent Maratha pride has initiated the renaming of many colonial icons in hope of edging out any reminders of its colonial masters. If you get lost looking for the Chatrapati Shivaji Maharaj Vastu Sangrahalaya, not to worry—sympathetic Mumbaikars will still direct you to the Prince of Wales Museum!

Sitting on a lush sculpture-strewn garden at what the British planners termed the Crescent Site across the Gateway of India, the Sangrahalaya was designed by a prominent architect named George Wittet. Almost 20 years after the building's foundation stone was laid in 1905, the four-storey museum opened in 1923.

The architecture of the building, quite like a fusion sampling platter, itself is a point of discussion. George Wittet's design, selected after an open competition, is a charming example of the Indo-Saracenic style which was an amalgam of Indian aesthetics and Western architecture. Look around the exterior and you will notice Moorish arches, Victorian towers and elements from Mughal palaces such as *jharoka*-like balconies, latticework, inlaid floors and a huge dome inspired by the Gol Gumbaz mausoleum down in Southern India. From the interior under the central dome is a balcony with railings and columns resembling an 18th-century *wada* (mansion) from Maharashtra, while the central pavilion is supported by intricate Jain-style columns.

The museum has over the last century amassed a sizably arresting collection of eclectic artefacts. It is a must-visit for its priceless pieces from India's 5,000-year-old ancient past, including those from the Mohenjodaro and Harappa Civilisations, painted manuscripts from *Laur-Chanda* dated between 1550 and 1570, and the *Anwar-i-Suhaili* painted in the court of Akbar.

Also impressive is the private collection of rare Japanese and Chinese artefacts from beyond its national borders. In addition, galleries are devoted to Indian sculpture, European paintings,

LOCATION:

Nearest stations: Churchgate and VT. Visitors can access the museum by BEST buses from both these rail terminals.

Open 10:15 am– 6 pm. Closed on Mondays.

Tantric-Buddhist art and some mundane natural history exhibits, notwithstanding an intriguing 20-ft-long saw fish caught in the nets off the waters of Bombay!

QUEEN'S NECKLACE

Walkers, courting couples, idlers, greyed citizens and families escaping the claustrophobia of matchbox living spaces spill onto Marine Drive and Chowpatty, their refuge from the schizophrenic pace of the city.

Back in 1940, when Marine Drive, the 'C'-shaped deep loop of the bay on the Western shore road was unveiled, complete with a 3 km sea-hugging promenade fronting a row of low-rise, art-deco style residential buildings, it became an instant icon.

Renamed in recent years as Netaji Subhash Chandra Marg, Marine Drive is the signature landmark of Mumbai today. The shoreline is lined with tetra pods installed in the 1970s to deter encroachments, but recent facelifts under the "Beautify Mumbai" campaign has seen the promenade's retiling and beautification with aesthetically-engineered bus shelters, benches and foliage.

Marine Drive on a monsoon-heavy day.

At sundown, if a Mumbaikar desires to witness the fiery orb slip into the blue expanse of the Arabian Sea, Marine Drive is the place to head. As the lights come on at dusk, Marine Drive magically morphs into a diamante-studded necklace adorning a dusky maiden, hence its christening as the Queen's Necklace.

Marine Drive starts out from the promontory on the southern-most edge of the promenade in front of Nariman Point. Sit on the wall's edge with your back to the noisy traffic and manic pace of life—all you will see is the sublime sight of uncluttered blue expanse of water speckled with tiny fishermen's dhows right out till the horizon.

Across the road, the prestigious National Centre for the Performing Arts (NCPA), Mumbai's theatre mecca, stands sentinel-like facing the sea, while the Bay View Bar located within Oberoi Towers along the NCPA stretch provides a five-star lookout in an ambience heady with live jazz and cigars.

As you walk north down the six-lane loop towards Chowpatty, Marine Drive relaxes. The crowd thins out and the landscape alters, revealing rows of bygone, blackened, dilapidated art-deco buildings, with a single elegant exception. The Intercontinental Hotel, an art-deco building cleverly converted into a hotel while maintaining the original façade specifications stands out as a spiffy, new corner block amongst the crumbling others. A hope for the Queen's Necklace's future rehab, maybe?

Linger not at this place though. Once on Chowpatty, the megapolis' oldest and original seafront, the action picks up again. Across the landmark one-and-a-half century old Wilson College, the beach, while not swim-friendly, is the true *pièce de résistance*.

Considered the Mumbaikar's outing delight—chaotic, loud and a hodgepodge, Chowpatty in the evenings is a city high on its dreams. A motley bunch of entertainers, miniature Ferris wheels, contortionists, magicians, astrologers, snake charmers and monkey keepers are all there hustling to attract customers. On odd days, the wide beach also serves as the unlikely venue for large religious and political congregations.

Since you are at Chowpatty, the outing cannot be complete without food. Latest Bollywood music blares out from street

food stalls located smack on the beach as waiters entice visitors to sample their delicacies. The famous Chowpatty Bhel is sold from Bhel Plaza, a setup with as many as 28 *bhelpuri* sellers. Simultaneously, *pav bhaji* (a bread and curry one-dish meal), *chaat*, ice-gola (sorbet-like, a Mumbai speciality), and *kulfi* also find their loyal customers.

Snake charmers add a carnival mood to Chowpatty Beach.

Those wary of sampling food here can take a short walk down to the private beach where the H20 Salt and Water Grill and Sports Complex, Bollywood actor Suniel Shetty's contribution towards a posh sport-themed dining alternative, is located. Just across the road is an equally eclectic array of choices, some so celebrated that they are a must-try. A *chole bhatura* meal at Cream Centre followed by a sweet *masala paan* from the vendor sitting outside the restaurant and dessert à la Wimbledon's strawberries with whipped fresh crème and vegan ice-cream at Bachelorr, a hole-in-the-wall eatery tucked along the railway lines…this is magic to be experienced!

♥ RAMZAAN **RAZZMATAZZ**

Pragmatism and sanity be damned. If it is Ramzaan, you should be in Mohammad Ali Road. The smokiness of meat roasting on fiery coal, the sugar-laced *malpuas* and fresh out-of-the-oven *nankhatais* from the bakery—all the action is here in these Muslims clusters called mohallas. Amongst the most famous mohallas are Nagdevi Street near Crawford Market, Minara Masjid and Bohri Mohalla. The best time to visit these mohallas is of course during the month-long period of Ramzaan when the whole place comes alive with fairy lights, night markets, restaurants and street food vendors that remain open throughout the night.

The area around Minara Masjid and Bhendi Bazaar is a mohalla worth a visit. The pistachio-green coloured minars of the Minara Masjid and the nearby madrasa (one of the 80 in the city) present the perfect photograph-taking opportunity. During the Ramzaan month, parts of the road in the Minara Masjid are converted into semi-pedestrian walkways where brisk nocturnal business transpires, with families hanging out at food stalls and shopping for garments and other bric-a-brac. Admittedly a bit harsh on the pocket, it is a particularly popular haunt for the affluent and the average, the finger-licking delicacies sold here attracting people from posh Breach Candy to plebeian Bhendi Bazaar. Suleiman Mithaiwala, a legend in these parts, stands at the entrance of the Minara Masjid alley offers desserts like *firni* and *mithais*.

Located beyond Minara Masjid, Bohri Mohalla is the place to spot the iconic Bara Handi Hotel (restaurant). Across the tomb of the late Bohra leader Syedna Tahir Saifuddin Saheb, you will notice the restaurant where customers are presented with a spread of *naans* and 12 cauldrons (*handis*) of delectable meat curries (*kormas*) and *salans* (dishes cooked in thick spicy *masala*). For those who care for local variants of cookies like *nankhatais*, *khari* biscuits and Zeera biscuits, the Makhadoom Sani Ashrafi Mohinuddin bakery, the oldest and most famous bakery in these parts, is also a Bohri Mohalla speciality.

A scintillating smorgasbord of sights, sounds and smells, this is one visit that should start with a statutory warning: injurious to your health. No, it is not the chaos in these precincts that is a concern, but the hazardous gastronomic overindulgence. But then again, Ramzaan comes only once a year!

ROCK-CUT CAVES OF MUMBAI

For all the glories bestowed on the colonial masters, Mumbai was neither a British find nor the Portuguese's eureka moment. No doubt, this was largely a swampy marshy archipelago of seven islands prior to the arrival of the enlightened western invaders. Trawl in deeper, though, and hidden behind the city's concrete clutter are five groups of spectacularly cut ancient rock caves that point vehemently towards the islands' existence as a vibrant place in ancient history as well.

Indeed, there was once a time between the first and ninth century when itinerant Buddhist monks used the seven islands as a working monastery, and the native populace were devout Shiva adherents. By all accounts, Mumbai was a thriving destination for trade and businesses even then, which perhaps attracted many dynasties and people to its shores.

All the five groups of caves found in the city are cut from the grey Basalt rock outcrop that abounds in this region. Some of the caves, like the 2,000-year-old Buddhist cave temples at Kanheri in the Borivli National Park (Sanjay Gandhi National Park) and the Kondivita or Mahakali caves in Andheri owe their genesis to the proselytizing Buddhist monks of Mauryan Emperor Ashoka's reign. Others are dedicated to Shiva, like the 1,500-year-old Mandapeshwar caves in Borivli East, the Jogeshwari cave complex, and the most famous of all, the Elephanta Caves, pointing towards the control that Shaivite dynasties like the Rashtrakuta and Silhara empires exercised over the city.

Awesome the caves are, but today most of the lesser-known ones lie neglected and have become a refuge for encroachers, mafia guys, drug addicts and even quick sex romps. The ones worth visiting are the Elephanta Caves, a UNESCO designated World Heritage Site well preserved even today, and the Kanheri Caves.

The magnificent entrance to the Elephanta Caves.

Elephanta Caves

Located 10 km out in the Sea of Oman is the Elephanta Caves, a must-visit for the mystical and spiritual vibe they exude. Standing in the main sanctuary and flanked on the sides by 20 fluted stone pillars, one can sense the palpable presence of craftsmen a millennium ago chiselling the basalt rocks into a monumental edifice in praise of their god, the omnipotent Lord Shiva.

> **LOCATION:**
> Gharapuri Island.
> Open from
> 9 am–5 pm.
> Closed on Mondays.
> Entrance fee for
> citizens of India is
> Rs. 10 per head,
> and for others,
> Rs. 250 per head.
> Admission is free
> for children up to
> 15 years of age.

Elephanta Island is a small 16-sq km round-shaped island nicknamed so because Portuguese explorers of the 17th century were greeted by a mammoth basalt stone elephant structure when they stepped onto this island. As with all other sculptures here, the Portuguese plundered the elephant. Later in 1864, the English tried moving the stone elephant, but failed and instead placed it at the Victoria and Albert Museum (now Dr Bhau Daji Lad Museum) in Mumbai's Jijamata gardens. Two huge cannons that you see atop the caves were also installed by the British to protect the Bombay harbour.

Originally called the Gharapuri Island (Island of Caves), Elephanta was once upon a time the Chalukya capital. It is believed that in the sixth or seventh century during the reign of the Chalukya and Rashtrakuta kings who were Shiva worshippers, Gharapuri's rock-cut cave temples were developed.

The layout of the Elephanta temple is simple. Hewn deep into the outcrop and covering 60,000 sq ft, there is a main chamber on the north-south axis along with two smaller ones located laterally on the east-west axis, beside some courtyards and other spaces.

Badly plundered by the Portuguese invaders who used the statues for target practice, Elephanta is not in a pristine state. Yet sculpturally it is breathtaking. Considered amongst the most spectacular pieces of Hindu rock-cut art, Elephanta has gargantuan images of Brahma, Shiva in his various avatars and his consort, Parvati.

Some amongst the many iconic rock-cut depictions of Shiva are the monolithic *shivalinga* (a round, phallus-like cylindrical statue that sits on a circular base symbolising the union of man and woman), Nataraja (Shiva performing the Cosmic Dance), Ardhnareshwara (Shiva's androgynous avatar), Andhakasuravada (Shiva killing demon Andhaka), his marriage to Parvati and

Shiva as the Mahayogi (the ascetic god). Yet the magnum opus relief is that of Trimurti Shiva, a 20-ft tall bust that depicts the three forms of Shiva—Aghora, the turbulent one; Tatpurush, the benign one and Vamadeva, the lovable one.

A day trip to the island is a pleasant one. Just an hour's boat ride from the Gateway of India, the Elephanta is forested with palm, mango, and tamarind trees, and monkeys abound in its wilderness. In terms of infrastructure, Elephanta is still very much semi-urban. A small population of 1,200 people inhabit the island, and you will see them in the precincts of the temple selling snacks, souvenirs and *jamuns* (tangy, purple berries). The locals run a narrow gauge train from the pier to the base of the temple steps and also offer palanquin rides for those who are unable to negotiate the 1,000 steps that lead up to the temple.

Interior of the Elephanta Caves, a World Heritage Site.

Kanheri Caves

Spartan and austere in their architecture because of Buddhist beliefs, the 101 caves of Kanheri are a fine example of the Buddhist lifestyle. About an hour's drive from South Mumbai, these caves are located in the hills of the Sanjay Gandhi National Park (Borivli National Park), which is more popularly associated with its animals than architecture.

From the 100 inscriptions in the caves in Devnagiri, Pallavi, Sanskrit and Brahmi script, it is known that the area was referred to as Krishnagiri, Krishnasila, Kanhasila or Kanhagiri, all translated to mean Black Mountain or Black Rock. Built by Buddhist monks, the Kanheri Caves seem to have started out as a rest stop for itinerant monks travelling between the

Carved sculptures at the Kanheri Caves.

ancient port towns of Sopara and Kalya in the third century BC, during Buddhist Emperor Ashoka's reign of Mumbai. These later evolved into a working Buddhist monastery.

Do not expect the flamboyance of the Elephanta Caves at Kanheri. While the 101 caves chiselled and carved out of a rough basalt outcrop is no small feat, they are frugal aesthetically. In its Viharas (caves that worked as rest houses), you will see coarsely-hewn stone beds and cisterns for water. A bit more elaborate are the Chaityas, or larger caves used for prayers, which are embellished with relief carvings of Buddha and Bodhisattvas. The most decorated is the 34-pillared main hall with a seven-metre-tall figure of a standing Buddha and an eleven-headed Avalokiteshwara, the compassionate lord of the world.

SARVAJANIK **GANESHOTSAV**

During the mid-monsoon period when Ganeshotsav arrives, the ten-day Hindu festival bathes the city in a melange of colour, music, ceremony and pageantry rarely witnessed on a scale as gigantic as this. Bollywood celebrities, political big-wigs, industrialists, families of the rich and poor, upper castes and untouchables all congregate to seek blessings from Lord Ganesha—the elephant-headed, wise child-god, the Vighnakarta (remover of all obstacles).

The tradition of Ganesh Puja has been recorded as far back as the reign of the Chalukya kings in the sixth century, but it was a simple family affair then. In its contemporary communal avatar, Ganeshotsav was first showcased in Bombay in 1893 when much to the British masters' ire, residents of Keshavji Naik performed a Sarvajanik Puja, or community festivities.

Organised against a backdrop of brutal British high-handedness during the Indian Sepoy Mutiny of 1857, the Ganeshotsav Sarvajanik Puja was meant to be a show of defiance against the British. Though the Indian Sepoy Mutiny had been crushed, the cry for freedom was gaining strength. Furthermore, Christian missionaries were furiously canvassing for English education, blinding the illiterates by their supposed superiority and dismissing the ancient glory, heritage and philosophy India was once known for on the world firmament.

Aware of the magnetism of religion and also of the expediency for refashioning Indian identity, Bal Gangadhar Tilak, Maharashtra's celebrated freedom fighter, called out to celebrate Ganeshotsav together at a community level. Tilak had already witnessed the success of similar community celebrations in a few other places, and found a perfect tool for bringing the community together. People hesitated. To stand up to the British was not an easy thought. Spurred by a respect for the erudite Tilak, middle-class educated Maharashtrian residents of the Keshavji Naik's chawl set up a Sarvajanik Puja *pandal* (tented community festival venue). Few else dared.

That year in all of Bombay, there was that one Sarvajanik Ganpati (another name for Lord Ganesha) Puja. By 2006, close to 9,000 Sarvajanik Ganesh *pandals* had celebrated Ganeshotsav, and approximately 1.5 lakh households brought idols of Ganpati home. Curiously, even today these Sarvajanik Pujas continue to

LOCATION:

Lalbaug Cha Raja Sarvajanik Ganeshotsav Mandal, Shree Ganesh Nagar, Dr Babasaheb Ambedkar Road, Lalbaug Market, Mumbai 400012
Tel: 24713626

be held in *pandals*, sometimes by the side of a road, in building compounds or at open grounds.

For months before Mumbai's biggest festival, statue makers across the city get busy with orders for crafting statues of Ganesha, some as tall as 20 ft. As the day draws nearer, intense competition ensues amongst mandals (festival committees) to bag the most innovative, exquisite and creative Ganapati statue for their Sarvajanik Puja. On the first day of Ganeshotsav, chants hailing the arrival of Lord Ganesha, *"Ganapati Bappa Mourya"* ring throughout the city. After a ceremonial welcome, the statue is installed on its pedestal.

Amongst all other Puja venues, the Lalbaug area is the colossus. Famed for its massive and opulent statues, Lalbaug hosts about a dozen idols every year, the most talked about for its scale of arrangements being the Lalbaug Cha Raja (King of Lalbaug) Sarvajanik Ganeshotsav mandal. The ten-day festival is run akin to a business enterprise. In 2007, it was rumoured that Lalbaug Cha Raja had a sanction to spend a three-crore kitty over the ten days, receiving close to two crore devotees and profiteering around eight crores! The mandal even secured a 25,000 sq ft area with metal detectors, CCTVs, volunteer security staff sporting walkie-talkies and other conveniences.

Visit you must, if not for the rituals, then to catch the varied depictions and interpretations of Lord Ganesha. The Mighty Ganesha shares stage space with idols of Harry Potter, the Indian cricket team or a Ganesha that is embellished with coconuts, chocolates or fizzy drink cans. Anything goes!

Ganeshotsav culminates on the tenth day, when the city-wide *visarjan* or immersion of the idols commences. Cries of *"Ganapati Bappa Mourya, Pudcha Varshi Laukar Ya"* (Lord Ganpati, please come back next year) echo in the city as lakhs of people come out on the streets of Mumbai singing and dancing to the beat of the drums and laziums.

Close to 200,000 Ganesha idols are taken in processions to one of the 25 lakes and water bodies present in Mumbai. Chowpatty is the most popular one. Families with their tiny Ganesha idols wade in the waters and amid chanting mantras, the idols are gently let go into the water. Of course, the mammoth statues get help from lorries and dhows to give them a deeper sea immersion!

Overleaf:
Worshippers
immerse Ganesh
idols into the sea
off Chowpatty.

SASSOON DOCKS

If you go past Colaba Causeway and further up across Colaba Market, you can smell it in the air: a fishy fetor emanating out from the Sassoon Docks.

The Sassoon Docks is Western India's first wet docks, constructed by Bombay's wealthiest merchant of the time, David Sassoon, a Baghdadi Jew whose family emigrated to India when he was still young.

The entry into Sassoon Docks is fraught with an access through a road rendered slippery with water dripping off trucks laden with fish baskets, handcarts, autorickshaws and even Koli women walking down to the Colaba market carrying the wicker fish baskets on their heads.

The main centre for offloading and trading fish in South Bombay, Sassoon Docks springs to life during the pre-dawn hours every morning as fisherfolk anchor in, bringing basketfuls of catch onto the harbour. It is an interesting sight watching such intense activity taking place at 5:30 am in the morning—fish baskets being flung with practised ease from the boat to the shores and then to the porters and other waiting fishmongers.

An auction of the fresh catch is the day's highlight, where you can catch agitated traders and fishmongers bargaining hard and tough for a good deal. Deal-brokering that ensues between the fisherfolk and the buyers is a rather aggressive and animated spectacle. Koli women, traditionally draped in their saree and gold jewels, are a garrulous lot, notorious for getting their way lest people have to face their acerbic tongue.

Such is the frantic paraphernalia and bustle of the place that Sassoon Docks made it into one of the episodes of the popular American reality series, *The Amazing Race*!

Displaying the day's catch at Sassoon Docks.

SEWRI MUDFLATS

Mumbai, a cradle of an ecological wonder. That doesn't seem to add up, does it?

Consider this: A choking megapolis with a 10-km long coast, home to 15 species of mangroves in a swamp nicknamed the Sewri mudflats. Surrounding it are heavy industries, shipbreaking yards and the city's only river, the Mithi River, polluted with unacceptable levels of effluents such as lead, mercury and chromium.

This ought to logically spell death in big, bold letters. But this quirk of natural and man-made circumstances has instead made the Sewri mudflats a haven for a whopping 150 species of birds such as egrets, brown-headed gulls, visitors from Central Asia including the Eastern Imperial Eagle and Oriental White-backed Vultures; and most special of all, the pink-coloured Greater Flamingos and the Lesser Flamingos.

In 1994, after a 40-year disappearance, the flamingos returned. With black-tipped pink beaks, pink spindle legs and a mid-flight wingspan brushed with black and pink, these beautiful birds completely altered the drab skyline. From October to March every year, the brown sludgy expanse of the mudflats is now swathed in a beautiful hue of pink when the flamingos arrive in droves. Early mornings, within an hour following high tide, thousands of birds flock the mudflats foraging for food, making

LOCATION:

Central Mumbai. Take the Harbour line train and alight at the Sewri Station, then take a taxi to the Colgate factory; from its vicinity the birds can be spotted. Alternatively, certain tour companies like Mumbai Magic (Tel: 9867707414) also conduct personalised tours to the area.

it a breath-stopping sight indeed.

These flamingos do not breed here and it is not quite known where they come from. Some believe they come from the Rann of Kutch in Gujarat where they also breed, while another commonly held belief is that these birds originate somewhere in Central Africa and cover a distance of 15,000 km before landing at Sewri.

Why the Sewri mudflats? Researchers, flummoxed initially by these flamingo arrivals, discovered unwittingly that due to the increase in swamp temperatures caused by pollution, coupled with the presence of algae and crustaceans, the flamingos' major food sources, the mudflats had become the perfect grounds for a hospitable stay for these birds!

When it quickly became obvious that this migratory pattern was not an aberration, the Mumbai Port Trust, the official custodian of ports and owners of large chunks of this mangrove land, declared the Sewri mudflats a protected ecology in 1996.

A city as bereft of ecosystems as Mumbai is, the flamingo spectacle has brought about a new awareness amongst its citizens to protect this fragile wonder. Corporate houses and individuals have been canvassing to provide a suitable home to these rare winged creatures, fearing that the proposed Mumbai Nava Sheva link mooted in 2007 to ease traffic bottlenecks in the city will threaten the fine ecological balance of Mumbai's wetland. Will human compulsions once again win the battle?

Pink-coloured Lesser Flamingos in the Sewri mudflats.

SIDDHIVINAYAK TEMPLE

If Mumbai is home to the glitzy rich and the grovelling poor, it is also home to the greatest emotional leveller—the Hindu Siddhivinayak Temple located in Prabhadevi at the busy intersection of Kakasaheb Gadgil Marg and S.K. Bole Marg.

On Tuesdays, at the crack of dawn, meandering queues of devotees armed with offerings of coconut and floral garlands throng the temple seeking blessings from Ganesha, son of Lord Shiva the Destructor and Goddess Parvati the goddess of wealth. Ganesha, the Elephant-headed god is in his most benign form considered the remover of all obstacles. Hindus customarily begin important events by invoking the blessings of the Lord.

Such is the temple's spiritual draw that devotees—Bollywood stars, business magnates, political hotshots and other lesser mortals—often walk barefoot throughout the night from different parts of the city to propitiate Lord Ganesha. The temple's website (http://www.siddhivinayak.org) makes mention of more than 10,000 devotees visiting the shrine every Tuesday.

However, the Siddhivinayak Temple is neither a designated Hindu pilgrimage nor a masterpiece. Its humble beginnings are traced back to a personal pledge of Mrs Deubai Patil, whose financial endowment saw its construction in 1801. The shrine, as originally planned, was a modest single-storey temple structure with a small 2' 6" tall black stone Ganesha, copied from an old calendar that used to hang in Deubai Patil's home. The calendar's image of Ganesha, it turned out, was copied from the Ganesha statue at Walkeshwar's Banganga temple.

The Siddhivinayak idol depicts Ganesha with four hands, each holding elements special to his divinity—a lotus, an axe, a rosary and a bowl of *modak*, the sweetmeat Ganesha is said to fancy. On either side, he is flanked by his consorts, Riddhi and Siddhi, thus the name Siddhivinayak.

What compels all of Mumbai to converge at this modest temple then? Unlike most other statues of Ganesha, the Siddhivinayak deity has his trunk pointing to the left side, and the general Hindu belief is that this particular version of the deity is more difficult to propitiate than the others, giving it a special significance.

LOCATION:
Shree Siddhivinayak
Temple Trust
Prabhadevi,
Mumbai 400028
Tel: 24373626
Website:
http://www.
siddhivinayak.org

With the Siddhivinayak Temple achieving cult status in the latter half of the last century, an expansion became imperative. In 1990 the temple underwent a massive makeover. At a cost of Rs. 30 million, a complete facelift was effected, rendering 21st century efficiency to the 18th century shrine.

Today, the sanctum around the idol has been enlarged and the temple sports a multi-angular, six-storey pink granite and marble façade crowned by a gold-plated dome. Interestingly, Hindu-Muslim antipathy notwithstanding, the wood carving of the sanctum's door frame was done by a Muslim artisan's family known traditionally for their intricate carving skills. This family had also worked on wood carvings at Mecca-Medina, the holiest of Muslim shrines!

Quite like most big temples, Siddhivinayak Temple charms a visitor not only with its spirit but also with a 24/7, carnival-like ambience around it. Vendors line both sides of the street leading to the temple selling exquisite garlands (some almost life-size) and offerings of coconuts and sweets. Brisk business is conducted at the stalls selling terracotta, stone and synthetic crystal deity statuettes, devotional music CDs and tapes, as well as a multitude of other ceremonial and religious paraphernalia. Given that the livelihoods of many families are generated out of this area, one government attempt not too long ago to ban the coconut and garland offerings due to a supposed security hazard was challenged heavily by vendors. Many of them, being migrants from elsewhere in India, fought hard to maintain their livelihood, subsequently forcing the government to revoke the ban.

The Siddhivinayak Temple is under a constant security risk. Keeping security concerns in mind, a large section of the temple precincts have of late been cordoned off. A bit of a dampener, but a magically divine experience nevertheless!

THE FORT WALK

LOCATION:
Fort area
Nearest station:
Churchgate

No one in the Fort area would pause to think: How awesome! After all, it is not the pristine Parisian or Victorian skyline one is looking at. Depending on which part you are in, there will be handcarts, BEST buses, ubiquitous yellow-and-black taxis, honking cars and motorcycles, on top of a few random cows and pedestrians.

Digest all of that. Then start all over again from the outer perimeter opposite the High Court on the intersection of R. Poddar Chowk and Karamveer Bhaurao Patil Marg. Bombay, the British presidency town, started out from this point with the wide Arabian Sea on its right and the formidable Fort walls on the left within which contained the British Sahib's township. Victorian, posh and sprawling, this was the late 1800s when the British, encouraged by a surging economy, aspired towards moulding the scattered island swamp into a showcase city.

As you look diagonally across to the right skyline you will begin to see Mumbai differently. Walk towards the edifices that seem shrouded by thick green foliage and you will soon be standing in front of a row of exquisite heritage buildings—the Mumbai High Court, the University of Mumbai, Rajabhai Tower and the Secretariat.

Global events in the mid-1800s had transformed the island-town into one of the most spectacular British presidency cities. The opening of the Suez Canal made Bombay into a port of reckoning. About the same time, the Indian Railways was launched, coupled with an increased demand for Indian cotton as a result of the American Civil War. Simultaneously, Sir Bartle Frere, the visionary with dreams of a modern, commercial and grand Bombay arrived. The Bombay skyline was about to change for good.

With the support of the city's planning body, the powerful Improvement Trust, Sir Bartle Frere engineered the removal of the Fort walls surrounding Bombay's township, opening up a clear view of the sea edge. The new landscape set the stage to establish a prominent physical manifestation of the British Empire.

Today, what you see here is largely a creation of Frere's vision. First in sight is the 1878-built Mumbai High Court

crowned with statues of Mercy, Justice and a few crosses. It is said that the British engineer who designed this building, General James Augustus Fuller, was tremendously inspired by the London Law Courts; compare pictures and there is great similarity indeed.

However, local artisans and masons were employed and given a carte blanche in the interior carvings. The building, made from local black basalt, covers 80,000 sq ft and has Venetian galleries replete, rather incongruently, with elaborate carvings of animals. Most notable among them are monkeys holding scales of justice and foxes donned in barristers' cloaks, all thanks to these artisans' imagination!

Next to the Mumbai High Court and across the famed Oval Maidan where Sunday cricket matches are played stand the buildings of Mumbai University—the Rajabhai Tower and library. Established in 1857 with a funding from well-known banker and "Cotton King" Premchand Roychand, the University and its library are amongst the earliest universities established in British India. Again Venetian-Gothic in its architecture, it is a must-see to appreciate renowned British architect Sir George Gilbert Scott's attention to intimate design.

Executed in buff coloured local stone, the building's façade is accentuated with multiple turrets, floral motifs and tall,

narrow archways. It also sports a spiral staircase following the same design. Stained glass, a running design theme of all colonial architecture, is present here as well with the convocation hall boasting a circular stained glass skylight depicting the 12 zodiac signs. Of course, the man whose generous donation made this possible—Sir Cowasji Jehangir Readymoney, is represented in an imposing statue placed at the front of the hall.

Equally interesting, especially for its likeness to London's Big Ben, is the Rajabhai Tower, located in the same university compound. The Gothic Revivalist clock tower, completed in 1878, is 280 ft high with two rooms at the square-shaped ground level. On the higher floors, the tower is octagonal. Right on top above the clock, its façade is guarded by eight stone statues representing various ethnicities of Western India in those days. Under the main spiral staircase peeping from the arches are sculpted heads of English literature's legendary Shakespeare and Homer. The clock tower alone cost a whopping Rs. 400,000, the sum donated again by Premchand Roychand. Rajabhai Tower is named after the Jain broker's mother, Rajabhai. Much like its halcyon days, even today its bells chime every 15 minutes, though no longer to the tune *"Rule, Britannia"*!

The University Library holds many priceless correspondences exchanged between eminent personalities of the Indian freedom movement such as Mahatma Gandhi, Subhas Chandra Bose, V.D. Savarkar, Lokmanya Tilak and Swami Vivekanand. Of equal importance is the library serving as an archive of original UN documents housed in a special section.

Once out of these two buildings, you will find yourself at the Old Secretariat standing at the end of Bhaurao Patil Marg, across the present-day civil and city courts. Built in a style similar to the others with arches and long verandas, the Old Secretariat completes this stretch of colonial office establishments.

THEATRE IN MUMBAI

Long before being showcased at the Ganeshotsav evenings and residential colony gatherings, theatre had been an active ingredient of India's social fabric, providing both entertainment and critique. Theatre in India traces its origin to the period between the second century BC and fourth century AD when the Hindu Sage Bharat wrote the *Natyashastra* (translated from Sanskrit it means Treatise on Drama).

While *nautanki*, *tamashas*, *ras-lilas* and *ram-lilas*, all variants of folk theatre's oeuvre, had been around in Mumbai for many generations, drama with its contemporary vocabulary was first initiated by Mumbai resident Rambhau in the late 1800s when he staged plays based on the *Puranas*, stories on Hindu philosophies and cosmology. A novelty then, Rambhau's plays triggered off a frenetic mushrooming of theatres like The Grant Road Theatre where plays, including musicals written by Poona's famous Marathi playwright Vishnudas Bhave, were performed. Curiously, plays enacted until the early 1900s had no women; boys and men were employed to play female characters!

Since then, a highly-evolved commercial and amateur theatre has grown in Mumbai. Between 1850 and 1950, Parsi theatre dominated the scene but simultaneously the freedom movement also gave Bombay's Marathi Theatre a fillip. In post-Independence Bombay, English theatre sprung up and Bombayites revelled watching plays by Ibsen, Shakespeare, Shaw and Pinter.

In later years, the experimental Chhabildas theatre movement, which started out of a school auditorium in Dadar, took non-Indian language theatre out of the cocktail circuits into regional languages to those Mumbaikars who loved their plays in Kannada, Marathi and Gujarati. As that movement petered out in the 1990s, the subsequent downswing of the theatre scene in Delhi meant an exodus of theatre personalities into Mumbai, injecting freshness into the Mumbai theatre scene.

Contemporary theatre aficionados see weekly plays performed to packed houses and newspapers are full of advertorials promoting plays in languages as varied as English, Hindi, Gujarati, Marathi, Kannada, Sindhi, Bengali, Malayalam and Telugu. From Shakespeare's *Macbeth* to Marathi Theatre's

Ghasiram Kotwal, every genre and style finds a keen and discerning audience amongst Mumbai's theatre goers. Do not be surprised if you find a familiar Bollywood actor on stage. Theatre and movies have always had an extremely symbiotic relationship and famous Bollywood actors such as Nasseeruddin Shah, Amol Palekar, Om Puri and Shabana Azmi have straddled both worlds with equal aplomb.

Mumbai also hosts many annual theatre festivals, like the extremely well-attended Prithvi Festival organised by the Prithvi Theatre, and the oldest theatre festival in India, Kamgar Natya Utsav, which is exclusively a workers' initiative conducted without any government or institutional support.

With so much happening, the performing spaces have become experimental and edgy. You could stage a play at experimental spaces like Prithvi Theatre, the Horniman Circle gardens or even the Bandra Bandstand sea promenade. You could also opt for the opulence of an elaborate premiere theatre space like the National Centre For Performing Arts, Sophia Bhabha Hall and the Shanmukhanand Hall.

Just as a visit to New York seems incomplete without a Broadway experience, so too would Mumbai not feel quite the same without an evening or matinee at its theatres.

WALKESHWAR

Walkeshwar is the place where you come across the intersection called Teen Batti or Three Lights, though there are no traffic lights in sight!

Until the 1990s property boom, Walkeshwar and the adjacent Malabar Hill had some of the most palatial, stately and secluded residences. Built around the 1930s and 1940s, they were owned by moneyed business families and *maharajas* from princely states.

Independence brought about dramatic changes to the city demographics. Sindhi migrants from Pakistan arrived, pushing the city's population from 1.49 million in 1941 to 2.3 million in 1951. Massive redevelopments became inescapable, sparing some exceptional buildings like the Raj Bhavan, the Maharashtra Governor's official residence spread over a lavish 49 acres of verdant jungle, rowdy waves and a cliff on the absolute edge. In olden times, pirates from Malabar clambered the cliff to pillage the settlements of the indigenous Koli natives. Alluding to this, the place came to be known as Malabar Point, and eventually became Malabar Hill.

Further fuelled by the booming fortunes of Jain diamond merchants operating out of Mumbai's diamond hub, avaricious property developers eventually razed several bungalows, erecting instead the Jain-dominated residential skyscrapers that you see dotting the Walkeshwar skyline.

Today, Walkeshwar has grown into a Jain cluster. For the uninitiated, Jains are followers of Jainism, one of the oldest religions in the world. Jains worship the 24 *Tirthankars* or saints, the last of them being the sixth century BC Lord Mahavira. Known sticklers for tradition and religious principles, these vegetarian worshippers believe in total *ahimsa* (abstinence from killing any living being) and an austere way of life.

It is said that where moneyed Jains abound, Jain temples are a given. Early morning, if you are in Walkeshwar you will be sure to spot Jain men and women on their way to the temple, a ritual they follow assiduously. Typically, a temple visit will see Jain men dressed in an ensemble of a white or cream drape and a *dhoti* (Indian sarong). Both men and women walk

LOCATION:
Babu Amichand Panalal Adishwarji Jain Temple Ridge Road, Walkeshwar (Malabar Hill), South Mumbai. Open daily from 5 am–9 pm

Carved columns in
Walkeshwar's Jain
temple.

barefoot (they believe they can sense insects coming under their feet and thereby avoid trampling them), and sport a *mupatti*, a white facemask-like fabric to avoid swallowing any air-borne organisms.

Similar to Hinduism in many ways, Jain rituals and ceremonies conducted in temples are interesting to watch. The deity is given a morning ceremonial bath amid chanting of mantras, the most important being the *naomkar* mantra, while devotees painstakingly create elaborate raw rice swastika (the Hindu symbol) motifs on low stools.

Walkeshwar boasts of three major Jain temples, all built by its wealthy Jain patrons. The oldest is the 1904-constructed Babu Amichand Panalal Adishwarji Jain Temple on Ridge Road. Ranked as one of the most beautiful temples in all of Mumbai, it is dedicated to Adinath, the first Jain *Tirthankar*, and also holds a black marble shrine of Parsvanath and another of the Hindu god Ganesha.

Quite unlike many other cacophonous places of worship, this temple is serenity personified. Intricately-carved marble pillars and *rajasthani*-style *jharokas* (balconies) adorn the outer façade while inside, the black-and-white concentric-patterned marble flooring is an aesthetic delight. Brightly painted jumbo-sized marble elephants flank the entrance to the sanctum, with the walls and ceiling also embellished with exquisite painted frescoes and carvings from the main events depicting the lives of the 24 *Tirthankars*.

There are other Jain temples in the same vicinity. One of the relatively newer shrines displays a multi-tiered marble circular pyramid depicting miniature painted statuettes of Hindu yogis (yoga practicing monks) working, one step a time, towards attaining a higher state of enlightenment, symbolised by the state achieved by the yogi on top tier of the pyramid—that *sadhu* is the Jain *Tirthankar* represented by a gold statue.

For the sheer serenity and calmness it offers, a Jain temple visit should be on every visitor's itinerary.

ZAVERI BAZAAR

Zaveri Bazaar has the highest concentration of jewellery shops in the city, and it is believed that Indian gold prices move largely according to the prices set here.

Sandwiched between Kalbadevi and Sheikh Memon Street sits Zaveri Bazaar, which has its origins in the 1860s when, invited by the British administrators, Gujarati and Marwari goldsmiths (Zaveri refers to goldsmiths) migrated into British Bombay and set up shop in this market area. Over the last 150 years, Zaveri Bazaar's sheen has remained the same. In fact, most of the families that set up businesses then still have their descendants operating out of this area.

In the random madhouse of a warren of lanes in Zaveri Bazaar there exist more than 1,500 jewellery shops. Along with stifling traffic, food vendors, diamond brokers and shoppers (mainly women of all ages) move in a sweaty surge hypnotised by shop windows displaying exquisite pieces of traditional jewellery. From a pair of gold earrings to a gold bridal jewellery set, Zaveri Bazaar knows how to seduce every customer.

Behind the main row showcasing the shops, you will find over 2,500 *karkhanas* (workshops) in the bylanes, where an estimated 15,000 artisans and craftsmen cram together producing exquisite gold and diamond jewellery. These jewellery coming out of the *karkhanas* also form a major part of the Indian jewellery export business. Estimates are that Zaveri Bazaar's gold transactions alone are worth $12.5 million every day. If the diamond business revenues are also included, the number would be topped up by an unbelievable $25 million dollars a day! In that context, Zaveri Bazaar plays a role far too critical to be ignored.

The pride of Zaveri Bazaar is no doubt Tribhuvan Das Bhimji Zaveri (TBZ), the bazaar's oldest and one of India's biggest jewellery chains which opened in these markets in 1864. Run by the fourth generation MBA-educated Zaveris, this store remains their flagship store, although the 143-year-old TBZ has branched all over the country. TBZ was the first to introduce air-conditioning in the shops and were also the first to employ female saleswomen in an industry which, until then, had been totally male-dominated.

The sun setting
upon Mumbai's
Juhu Beach.